HARRY TRUMAN

A POLITICAL BIOGRAPHY

HARRY TRUMAN

A POLITICAL BIOGRAPHY

———※———

By

WILLIAM P. HELM

Duell, Sloan and Pearce = New York

Introduction

———— * ————

BETWEEN many senators of the United States and their home state newspaper correspondents at Washington there exist strong personal attachments. For somewhat more than ten years such was the relationship between Harry Truman and myself. The period spanned the decade of his senatorship and the few months thereafter when he was Vice President.

In those years I came to know him well—better, I like to think, than any other correspondent in the Press Galleries of Congress. He was my warmest friend and best news source in the Senate. A prince of good fellows, he was gracious without condescension, always helpful, considerate, and good-humored. His head underwent no swelling during our long friendship; his big heart grew larger.

The general public knew relatively little of Harry Truman until he was projected, against his personal desires, into the second highest office in the nation. It was my privilege to follow his career intimately from the day of his arrival in Washington as Senator-elect.

[v]

This narrative therefore is intensely personal. It is as informal as was our relationship. In some measure it may be helpful in appraising, from his record, the man who rose in little more than a decade from small-town obscurity to the Presidency of the United States.

When Harry Truman was a fledgling senator I was impatient with him many times for his self-deprecation. He had asked me when I first met him to show him the ropes and I probably annoyed him frequently thereafter by my plain speaking. If so, he never indicated his annoyance. I felt then I was serving him, and I wanted to be of service. For he impressed me as no other senator ever did. He was so altogether unspoiled and human, so keen in his understanding of human traits and foibles, so charmingly outspoken and frank; and, withal, one of the most popular men ever to enter Congress.

On the day of his return to Washington after his re-election in 1940, for instance, he was given a miniature ovation by his colleagues of both political parties. They behaved like boys greeting a popular schoolmate who had just got over the measles. At the impromptu luncheon they immediately tendered him, they sang his praise in lusty song and no doubt their hearts were in the business as well as their vocal chords.

It would be easy to write about Harry Truman as only his press agent would write; there is so little in his record that isn't revealing of his folksy fellowship. This temptation has been resisted in the pages that follow. In his political philosophy he advocated nearly everything I opposed. I was his "black Republican" friend always, but no less his friend.

HARRY TRUMAN: A Political Biography

It was Harry Truman's unexpected fate to reap as President the harvest of policies he helped to implant as Senator. He doubtless has found the harvesting much more difficult than the sowing. But when he sowed, he never intended to harvest as President. At Chicago, in 1944, it was Harry Truman who really was drafted, rather than Franklin Roosevelt.

W. P. H.

HARRY TRUMAN

A POLITICAL BIOGRAPHY

———————✶———————

Chapter One

===============*===============

I WAS pounding my typewriter like the devil one day when I looked up and there in my office stood the thirty-third President of the United States.

"Hello," I said. "Have a chair. I'll be with you right away."

He sat down and I turned back to my machine. It was a swell story I was writing; something, I recall vaguely, about Edgar Hoover and what he was doing in the current murder mystery in Kansas City. As the Washington correspondent of the *Journal-Post,* I was letting the paper have the hot news fast. I was really going to town. It was too near the main edition deadline to entertain a visitor or even to think of one. Postal Telegraph messengers were dashing in and out, running the stuff as I wrote it. I had a direct wire to the news editor's desk.

The battered alarm clock on my desk ticked off the deadline. I had the knowledge sweet to newspapermen of knowing the editor would hold the edition for all of my story. So I blithely kept on writing. Soon it occurred to me, however, that I had to live with Johnny Johnsen, the news editor on the other end of the wire, day in and day out. And I knew it wouldn't make for future close harmony if I got his old Swedish goat by holding the edition up too long.

So I cut the story off about five minutes after I should have done so. Then I pushed back my chair and looked around. The thirty-third President was still sitting, his eyes twinkling, where I had waved him. I had forgotten him as completely as if he were out of this world. So I went over to make amends.

Only he wasn't the thirty-third President then. He was Missouri's junior senator-elect, and he was grinning like two Chessie cats. The time was a month or six weeks after Election Day of 1934. I had never seen him before and I wasn't expecting to see him then. I didn't know him.

"You're Bill Helm, aren't you?" he asked as we shook hands. "Well, I'm Harry Truman. Just got in town and thought I'd drop in and pay my respects."

All of a sudden the *Journal-Post's* Washington Bureau, consisting solely of myself, was in confusion complete and upsetting. Here, practically in my lap, was the new senator from the great State of Missouri—if you don't think it's great ask any Missourian—come to call. Come to "pay his respects," if you please, to a little viper of the press; and the viper hadn't even known him and had kept him waiting.

Only one thing occurred to me as suitable apology.

"Let's have a drink," I said. "I know a place—"

Harry Truman's grin widened. He wasn't at all offended. "Not now," he said. "Some other time. Just thought I'd get acquainted today. Let's talk."

[4]

So we sat down again. I was still uneasy, for it was no fitting place, I well knew, to entertain a senator. My dirty little office on the second floor of the old Maryland Building, now mercifully razed for the good of the city, was certainly the smallest and probably the dirtiest in the whole dingy place. It was flanked on the west by a chain-tailor company's suite of rooms almost as dirty as my own. These were run by a wag named Weller. His usual greeting to me of a morning was, "Well, how the Helm are you today?" I finally choked that corn off by answering, "Weller, thank you."

It was Weller's frequent failing to stand in my doorway when I had a caller. With an eye to business, he measured my visitors mentally for coat and pants; once he caught one of them and sold him a suit. As Truman and I started to talk, Weller appeared on the threshold. He looked at me and lifted his eyebrows.

"Beat it," I told him in a stage whisper. "Nothing doing."

He gave me a mocking bow and retreated. When Truman could no longer see him, out in the corridor, he saluted me by putting his thumb to his nose and went muttering back to his den. The next day he wanted to know why I had high-hatted him. I told him my caller had been Senator Truman of Missouri. He grunted.

"So what?" he beefed. "Roosevelt buys my suits. Why shouldn't Truman?"

In those lean days the tailoring business was bad and Weller wasn't overlooking any bets. He really did sell suits to the President. Before Truman became President, however, Weller died. Had he lived, he probably would have gone after Truman's trade.

[5]

To the east my office was bordered, as I recall it, by the lack-luster lair of a loan shark. The southern exposure was dominated by a window whose cracked panes hadn't been washed in the three years of my tenancy preceding Truman's visit. This window, however, wasn't a total loss. It was unequaled, for instance, for viewing an eclipse of the sun, superior by far to smoked glass. Just under it was a sloping roof the top of which collected dust and dirt from a bus terminal below. The reason for this, I found out, was to deposit it on my desk when I raised the window.

This unusual place was not my first choice as a setting for my labors. In fact, it was my last. I rented it for several reasons. As a man with a wife and four youngsters in the halcyon days of the Great Depression, I had practically no money for renting anything. The money all went for such gimcracks as victuals and shoes. Moreover, the Maryland Building's owners weren't too fussy about getting their rent on the first day of each month. If a hard-up tenant didn't come through for a spell, they let live.

That was the first reason. The others don't matter.

My office ad of tough times was unnoticed by Harry Truman. He had felt the nip of the wringer himself. What a man wore, the elegance of his office, and the bulge of his wallet mattered little to the new Senator from Missouri. If a man's face were reasonably clean and honest, that man generally looked all right in Truman's eyes. I learned later that Truman regarded every man as a gentleman until he showed up as another package. This trait cost him dearly at times in his senatorship when he vouched for shadies he had thought honest. Even these distressing incidents didn't sour the milk of his human kindness. His precept was: I respect everybody until I am shown my respect is not deserved.

We sat and talked in my dingy little office for perhaps half an hour. He was house-hunting, he said, expecting to bring his wife and daughter to Washington for the congressional session to start in January. Did I happen to know where he could get an apartment? Nothing pretentious, but just a good, comfortable place to live. But please go to no trouble about the matter if I didn't; he had plenty of time to go around to the real estate crowd and find something himself.

His voice was soft and his speech was homey. It was only when he dropped his grin, and such periods were infrequent and short, that I recognized him from pictures printed in the *Journal-Post*. There were charm and good humor in his face that eluded the cameras of those days even as color eluded them. And he had two qualities in measure so overflowing that none of his colleagues came near to matching them. These were his astonishing frankness on any subject under the sun and his colossal modesty and self-deprecation.

"I came to see you first of all," he told me to my embarrassment, "because you are a famous newspaperman and know all the ropes at Washington. You see, I've been reading your stuff in the *Journal-Post*. I thought maybe you wouldn't mind helping me find my way around."

When I protested, his answer was that he was "only an humble member of the next Senate, green as grass and ignorant as a fool about practically everything worth knowing."

Of course, he was kidding me, and I said so. "No such

thing," he declared crossly, running his words together. He toppled his grin so fast I could hear it crackle as it fell.

Here, I thought, is the eighth natural wonder of the world, a politician who doesn't take himself too seriously; a friendly, likable, warm-hearted fellow with a lot of common sense hidden under an overpowering inferiority complex. In the years I knew him as Senator, I never fully changed that appraisal. When he became Vice President, he lost some of his self-deprecation. And when he became President he had to part with what remained. He realized there's no such thing as a President with a habit of belittling himself.

But sometimes I wonder if he has really lost it all. It would seem a pity; he enjoyed it so much.

It used to pop up in such unexpected ways and places. At one stage of his senatorial career we had luncheon together fairly often. He would be host one time and I the next. We both liked a cocktail as a starter; and cocktails aren't served at Senate restaurants. So once in a while we would slip away from Capitol Hill downtown to Peter Borras' Madrillon restaurant where we could have a good drink.

Peter had pioneered a mild drink he called the Madrillon cocktail. We used to take two apiece while waiting for our food to come on the table, and never turn a hair. A third, however, was wont to swell my self-importance.

Once I ventured a fourth. Its effect was stupendous. My thoughts were brilliant and they flowed easily, naturally, and as rapidly as the waters of a flash flood. I had the whole solar system by the tail and made it revolve around me.

[8]

One day Truman and I had two apiece at Peter's restaurant and as our luncheon hadn't come along then, and as there was no special merit in waiting for it idly, we ordered a third. I succeeded in hiding mine—because I had work ahead that afternoon—and slipped it before Truman after he had drunk his. I then managed to get his empty glass in front of my plate without attracting his attention.

"Better drink your cocktail, Harry," I suggested.

When he looked down, pleasurable surprise flowered on his face. "I thought I had," he said. "That was the last one," I told him. So he drank it.

It was his fourth. Nobody was trying to get anybody else tipsy, but I knew what a fourth had done to me; maybe a fourth would do the same thing to Truman. I waited in vain; no change.

Then I was overcome by inspiration.

Surely, I thought, five of these delicious little things will make my good friend self-assertive; why, they ought to blast his self-deprecation to atoms. So I mentioned, very casually I thought, that I'd like another cocktail and would he join me? He shot a quick, quizzical glance my way and said he really didn't care for any more. So I called Martin and ordered two more.

Truman drank Number five. Now, I thought, he will find out for once in his life what a good man he is. He didn't. I tried to wangle my full glass before him again but wasn't quick enough and he caught me in the act. I told him I'd changed my mind and didn't want it; would he please not let it go to waste?

"You old son of a gun," he said, "I believe you ordered it just because you thought I wanted it."

[9]

And down his hatch it went.

And then I knew by all that was good and true that he would find himself, that his overwhelming modesty would vanish. He was cold sober, as ever, but I thought I could detect a warming glow in his manner. He placed his hand in friendly fashion on my arm.

"Bill," he said, "I'm having a good time. And I just want you to know I think it's mighty fine of you to be so kind to a practically unknown United States Senator!"

Once in his suite in the Senate Office Building, Truman served me there with a highball that was perfection, no less.

"Like it?" he asked, his face beaming. "All right, you old black Republican, I'm going to give you a bottle to take home. Here it is."

The label on that bottle was something to see: "From the Private Stock of T. J. Pendergast. Ten Years Old."

Truman's close friends enjoyed Tom Pendergast's Private Stock before Truman moved out of Suite 240 to go downtown to the White House. And while I heard criticisms aplenty of Pendergast himself, I have yet to hear a noble senator raise his voice against the quality of Pendergast's liquor.

Early in his senatorial career Truman was admitted to a little group of good fellows, all colleagues, who liked a toddy in mid-afternoon. This fondness was apt to interfere with business. The Senate frequently dallied long past three o'clock; to go back to the Office Building for a drink meant missing proceedings on the floor certainly for a quarter of an hour, maybe much longer.

Colonel Ed Halsey was Secretary of the Senate in those days. He was a convivial fellow himself. His inner office was only a ten-second stroll off the Senate Chamber and it had supplies for the thirsty. Only senators went through his doorway; here in privacy a suffering statesman could get the shot he craved. ·

And here Harry Truman strolled from time to time. One stroll, one drink, was his rule. But some of his cronies strolled more than once per afternoon and took more than one per stroll. I have seen them come back with flushed faces and thick tongues to the Chamber. From my perch in the Press Gallery I have enjoyed the vexation of their cold-sober colleagues, have seen kindly efforts to make the souses shut up or get out so the public galleries would not realize that the Demon Rum was on the floor below.

But with Harry Truman, never so. Ten years I knew him as one close friend knows another. Not once did I ever see him under the slightest influence of liquor.

One of his favorite and respected companions was Jack Garner, "Cactus Jack" from Texas, Vice President for six years of Truman's senatorial term. "The V. P.," Truman called him. It was Garner whom John L. Lewis, the mine workers' union head, publicly dubbed "a poker-playing, whiskey-drinking, labor-baiting, evil old man." Garner is said to have laughed heartily when he heard it, but Truman didn't think it funny. Truman's feathers stood up straight when anybody spoke unkindly of his friends.

Garner's inner office likewise had first aid for the thirsty. This he diluted with what he called branch water from a tap in his washroom. Truman was an infrequent caller there; so infrequent for a time that each occasional visit seemed to stand out in his thoughts to be mentioned proudly as a special event.

Sometimes Truman's poker-playing group had Garner with them. All senators, they used to get together once in a while in the evening. Garner seldom lost; it was common knowledge that he played his cards exceedingly close to his vest.

"I nicked the V. P. last night," Truman told me gleefully one day. Apparently "the V. P." had nicked him on previous nights.

One of Truman's favored poker games was seven-card stud. This he played with the skill of the average player, often paying the penalty of misplaced confidence in his cards just as he sometimes paid another sort of penalty for misplaced confidence in men. Whether it was cards or men, he was a good loser.

There came a time in the latter part of Truman's first term when his fast pace of living began to tell on him. His workday usually started at seven o'clock in the morning when he came in, the first of the Senate's early risers, to his desk. Early to rise was a habit he had formed as a farmer's boy. Its complement, early to bed, he forgot as a senator.

He used those precious morning hours to prepare for the work ahead. A prodigious reader, he frequently would call on the Congressional Library for all it could send him on legislation in which he was closely interested. Such contributions were heavy. From seven o'clock in the morning until nine, when his office staff showed up for work, Truman digested these masses of heavy reading matter. A fact once stored in his retentive memory stayed there, and he became exceedingly well informed on bills before him.

But he didn't go to bed early much of the time. When there was no diversion in the evening, he drove home to the meal prepared by his wife and helped her by drying the dishes thereafter.

Most of the time he burned the candle at both ends.

"What's the matter with our Harry?" I asked Vic Messall, Truman's private secretary, one day. "He has got black rings under his eyes and his face is seamed and drawn."

Messall watched over Truman with doglike devotion. My question's import was mirrored by the worried look on his face.

"I know it, Bill," Vic replied. "And I know why. He's working too hard, playing too hard, and I think he's drinking more than he ought to. Not more than would be all right for him, you understand, when he isn't under such a strain of work, but more than he ought to right now when everything is on top of him.

"I'm going to get him out of Washington and send him back to Missouri for a little rest."

Just that is what Vic did. When Truman returned he was in top form again.

Victor Messall was succeeded by Harry Vaughan as Truman's secretary and the two Harrys, Truman and Vaughan, sometimes indulged together. The war was on at that time and both had a burning desire to get into the thick of it. Both were Reserve Officers. Vaughan realized his ambition. He was given a commission as Lieutenant Colonel and ordered to Australia.

Truman openly envied him.

"I tried my damnedest to get into it myself," Truman told me. "But those old fuddy-duddies down at the War Department wouldn't let me. They said I could be of greater service here in the Senate which, of course, I don't believe. And now they've given Harry his commission and denied me mine."

When the time came for Vaughan to go, Truman rode across the continent, to San Francisco, to see him leave.

"I hope he comes back soon," Truman said on his return to Washington. "I couldn't miss my right arm more. And what do you think, Bill? We made an agreement that neither of us would take a drink until we meet again!"

That was a solemn agreement; both realized there was a possibility they might never meet again. To the best of my knowledge, Truman kept his pledge.

"Had a drink yet?" I asked him from time to time.

"Not yet," was always his reply. Sometimes he would add, "I certainly hope Vaughan gets back soon."

Vaughan wanted to see front-line service. Did he? I asked.

"Hell, no," Truman answered. "Do you know what they did with him? They took him to Australia and made him an Army policeman; Provost Marshal, which is another way of saying chief of police for all the U. S. troops in Australia.

"Harry's so disgusted he's half sorry he went into active service. I've had half a dozen bellyaching letters from him. But he's a good soldier and does what he's told to do."

A bit later it was Colonel Harry Vaughan and he re-

[14]

turned to the States and Washington and Truman's office. Truman was Vice President and it was Brigadier General Harry Vaughan, Military Aide to the Vice President. Later still it was Major General Harry Vaughan; that by the special grace of old friend Harry Truman. The Major General changed his address to The White House, Washington, D. C., where he was the beloved Military Aide of the President of the United States.

When Harry Truman became Vice President his ability to put a modest cargo aboard without listing came in handy.

By tradition, the Vice President is the capital's own social gadget, democracy's priceless boon to Washington Society. He is required, of course, to waste a few hours every week in presiding over the Senate. Something may be done about this in time. But all other hours of day or night, the Vice President is fair game and there is no closed season for the sport.

Harry Truman was a willing gadget. His immediate predecessors weren't.

Jack Garner lived quietly at a downtown hotel for the eight years of his Vice Presidency and set his beetling brows against all after-dark social affairs. His wife was his private secretary and shared his dislike for Society's fuss and feathers.

Henry Wallace went along with tradition in a serious way, stiffly and formally, without spontaneity.

When Harry Truman succeeded Wallace, the dowagers, matrons, and other formal entertainers and diners-out in the capital were over-ripe for an oldtime Vice President who could mix and like it. Harry Truman, prince of mixers, was their dish.

Washington Society took the Trumans to its hungry heart and Harry loved it. He snuggled close, was ever ready for another party. He went with quip and jest and wholesome zest. Bess Wallace Truman acceded graciously, although it was suspected now and then that she wasn't so enthusiastic about the new way of living as her distinguished spouse.

Margaret Truman, their only child, was not often in the picture. She was finishing her education at a local college and preparing for a stiff regime in voice training in New York. I suspect she sometimes longed for the gayer life to which her father turned so naturally. Years before, he once had told me that she was teasing him to take her to a White House reception. That was when Franklin Roosevelt was President.

"Why not give the kid a break and take her?" I asked.

"No," Truman replied, "she's too young. She's only fifteen, you know. And, besides, her mother has decided against it."

Mrs. Truman did not care for alcohol. Her feeling on the subject, which I think was rather casual so far as other persons were concerned, was known to the ladies of her social set when her husband was senator.

One night my wife and I were at dinner with a congressman and his wife at the Willard. Cocktails had just been served when the congressman's wife, a quick-witted lady as charming as she was pretty, placed her drink with evident agitation behind her glass of water, then nervously set it before Mrs. Helm.

"I've just seen Mrs. Truman," she whispered, "and I think she is coming our way. She wouldn't approve, and I don't want to distress her. So, please, it's yours."

Mrs. Truman did not come our way, and a few minutes later the lady retrieved her beverage. Her husband, who knew Truman well, mildly reproved her for her agitation.

"Mrs. Truman would have thought nothing about it if she had seen it," he said. "But you can bet she would have been puzzled if she had seen two cocktails before Mrs. Helm and none before you."

The numerous social functions that Truman attended as Vice President caused him to gain weight. It became him. And despite the long hours he seemed more rested and in better health in those days than at any time before or since during his stay in Washington.

"You seem to thrive on the treatment," I mentioned one day. "There's no need to ask you if you enjoy it."

"Yes, Bill, I do," he said. "I'm having a good time. Who wouldn't? Sometimes I have to eat more than I really care for. But I'm thoroughly enjoying it."

The swirl of entertaining ended abruptly on April 12, 1945. That was the day Franklin Roosevelt died. Since then I have not seen Harry Truman often. To many an old friend he is the prisoner of the White House. This cannot be helped; the President of the United States is servant of all its people. He cannot claim his own time to be spent in his own way. His time is the nation's.

Much of it must be spent formally in the pomp and

[17]

dignity befitting the world's foremost political leader. I sometimes wonder if Harry Truman, the most informal and democratic senator I ever met, wouldn't be glad to swap a week with one of his old Senate pals and know what it means again to come and go as he wishes. In a sort of way he tried to do just that—come and go as he wished—in his early days as President.

But it wasn't the same as it had been. Not by a reservoir-ful.

On those occasions he would run up to the Capitol to join his former colleagues of the Senate at luncheon in the Secretary's office. His host of those days, Colonel Halsey, was dead, Leslie Biffle had succeeded him as Secretary. Truman was fond of "Biff" and Biff gave the parties now. They were no longer just a few minutes of relaxation; food was brought in and the Big Shots of the Senate gathered and sat down to the board. Secret Service men were as numerous as grasshoppers in haying time and stood here, there and almost everywhere in the corridors.

Truman had a host of humbler friends when he was Senator—newsmen, guards, messengers, and clerks. Half the personnel in the Capitol knew and liked him. When as Senator he trod the marble floors he had a greeting for all, a handshake for many. But when he came as President to the Capitol, these old friends were stayed at a distance and glimpsed him generally only when he passed by.

"It's like moving a circus for me to go anywhere," the captive Truman complained.

Many things changed for Truman the night he was sworn in and said from the fullness of his heart, "I ask only to be a good and faithful servant of my Lord and my people."

And not all those changes made for his happiness.

Before that night his habits, his way of living, his spontaneity were his own business. Now they were everybody's. They were in the spotlight now of unpitying publicity that beats down upon the nation's head. Little stories concerning the trivial affairs of his life became big stories all of a sudden; little incidents were blown up like over-inflated balloons.

The American press, never too kind to Presidents, now wanted to print all it could about him, about what he did, what he said, how he carried himself. It bored like an intruding gimlet into his past, digging into all things relating to him and his affairs.

Truman had foresight, perhaps, of this when he asked again and again not to be nominated for the Vice Presidency. As senator, he had met the press and found some of it not to his liking. Even in those days he was inclined to attribute to the whole press the annoying tactics of its saffron segment.

But he wasn't embittered. He felt that as a man in public life he was a fair target for publicity. He felt that his family was not such a target. They were his wife and daughter and they were not a part of his public life. He resented persistent efforts to publicize their personal affairs. And he resented this no less when he became President.

And he knew the sort of so-called news about himself that some of the editors craved.

"When you go to the White House," one Washington

correspondent was instructed by his boss, "I want you to find out all you can about Truman's drinking parties. I hear he drinks like a fish. Find out what he drinks. Find out how much. Find out who puts him to bed when he gets tight. Let me have all you can get on it."

The newsman protested.

"All right," the editor agreed, "I know it isn't a very attractive assignment. But keep your eyes and ears open and let me know what you learn."

A short time later the correspondent resigned; "in disgust," he told me.

No editor was ever sold a worse pup than that bum tip. There is that sort of editor, of course. But there isn't that sort of President in the White House so long as Harry Truman is there.

Whether Truman heard of that particular assignment, I do not know. But what I do know from his own lips is his conviction that a part of the American press has never given him a break. He feels that some newsmen are sent to the White House to dig up scandal rather than news.

Chapter Two

———————————✳———————————

"IF IT hadn't been for Boss Pendergast, Harry Truman would never have been President of the United States. Pendergast gave him his start."

I wonder how many thousands of persons have said that. In part it's true; as a whole it may not be. It implies, for instance, that Pendergast was the sole architect of Truman's fortune; and that certainly isn't true. Many events and many persons other than Pendergast helped Harry Truman on his way to the White House.

To point to a single event in a man's life and say, "That made him what he is today," is to cover a lot of territory that has been neither mapped nor explored. It assumes possibilities that simply can't be taken for granted.

Old man Hanks, let's say, was quick on his feet, so quick that he dodged the arrows of a certain Indian. Hanks had a daughter, Nancy. Nancy meets Tom and from their union springs Abe Lincoln. Lincoln frees the slaves. Therefore, if old man Hanks hadn't been quick on his feet the slaves wouldn't have been freed.

It sounds specious, doesn't it?

Undoubtedly Pendergast's choice of Harry Truman as candidate for Senator from Missouri in 1934 did have much to do with Truman's becoming President. It may have been the chief reason why he became President, but it certainly wasn't the only reason. There were many others, near and remote. One was something that happened in Baltimore in the summer of 1912. From that happening a chain of circumstances ensued; if they had not developed as they did, Truman might never have entered the White House except as a visitor or a sightseer.

Again, a chance conversation in Truman's office in 1940 resulted in his attaining prominence as a Senate investigator. If he hadn't been a good investigator, if he hadn't made a reputation as such, he might not have been chosen by Roosevelt as his running mate in 1944.

Go back a bit, and we find that Truman bossed the building of a fine highway system in his home county. He bossed it well. If he hadn't bossed it well, he might not have had a chance with Pendergast when Pendergast picked the senatorial candidate.

And so on and on. It's a sort of House-that-Jack-built story. Indeed, so many things helped Truman to become President that no one has a prior lien on the others.

It is impossible to estimate even the number of persons who exercised direct influence on Truman's becoming President. To single out Pendergast is to overlook entirely the abilities and aspirations of Truman himself. Even his enemies admit he had a little something to do with his being in the White House. Some of his close friends feel that the chief reason Truman became President was Harry Truman.

Tom Pendergast gave him a nomination; eventually Truman went to the White House. A generation earlier Woodrow Wilson was given a nomination by Jim Smith, Democratic boss of New Jersey; and eventually Wilson went to the White House. To say that Truman would never have been President except for Tom Pendergast is like saying Wilson would never have been President except for Jim Smith. Maybe so, but who knows?

Wilson might have made it without Smith's start; and Truman might have made it without Pendergast's. For Truman had all the essential background and much of the know-how. He hailed from a politically doubtful state with fifteen electoral votes. He was a Democrat. During the Civil War his family's sympathies were with the Confederates, thereby providing him with the basis for the sympathy of the dominant southern wing of the party. He came from a section, however, that remained with the North during the war. He was of pleasing personality, a vote-getter, and clean. And when he won local office he administered it honestly and well.

All of which is put in the past tense because it relates to the Truman of 1934 standing on the threshold of his national career. Of such sturdy qualities and with such background do successful politicians spring.

Beyond the borders of his own Jackson County, Truman was almost unknown in 1934 and that, of course, was a handicap. It was a handicap that Tom Pendergast helped remove.

Two years before Truman was nominated for Senator, I met a congressman from Kansas City named Joseph B. Shannon. Shannon first was elected to Congress in 1930. In 1932, I became the Washington correspondent of his home-town paper, the *Journal-Post*. I learned about Truman first of all from Shannon.

Shannon was an old-school politician of strong likes and dislikes, a kind-hearted, friendly man in his middle sixties. At Washington he was rather lonely and I spent much time with him. He thoroughly disliked the *Star*, Kansas City's dominant paper. The *Star* claimed to be independent but veered strongly toward Republican philosophy. On its side, of course, were all the city's best people—well, nearly all. On Shannon's side were all the votes—well, an overwhelming majority, anyhow, in his congressional district.

In local politics the *Star* was on the outside looking in, and Shannon was on the inside looking out contemptuously at the *Star*.

The *Journal-Post*, underdog in the competition, also professed to be independent. On general principles it opposed nearly everything the *Star* advocated. Consequently it was far more sympathetic than the *Star* toward the Pendergast organization. Indeed, the fact that the *Star* fought Pendergast and all his works was almost enough in itself to put the *Journal-Post* on Pendergast's side. As a natural result, the Pendergast crowd was much more friendly to the *Journal-Post* than its strong competitor.

From the feud I profited as a correspondent. Shannon favored me with news items and took grim satisfaction in helping me scoop the *Star*.

He called me "Brother Helm." We had a common interest in which I shared lightly, he mightily. This was the study of Thomas Jefferson's life. He studied it as an admirer; I as a critic. On Jeffersoniana he was exceedingly well informed. He used to make a speech to the House every year on Jefferson's birthday and took great pride in being what he called a Jeffersonian Democrat. Often he railed at me pleasantly because I wasn't.

"Meet Mr. Helm of the *Journal-Post*," he frequently would say in introducing me to visiting bigwigs from Missouri. "I must warn you about him, however. He's a Republican from Virginia. He comes from a beautiful little town, Warrenton. I've been there as the guest of my dear old friend, Tom Payne, whose father fought in the Confederate Army. You remember Tom Payne, of course, when he lived in Kansas City. A sterling man and a sterling Democrat.

"Well, sir, when I was in Warrenton I went out with Tom Payne to the cemetery. And there I saw the honored graves of Mr. Helm's father and grandfather, and the graves of his uncles. They were decorated with the Confederate Cross. Mr. Helm's people fought in the Confederate Army. They were all good Democrats. And how in the hell a man with that background can be a black Republican is more than I can understand."

Having thus denounced me with twinkling eyes he then would take the curse off.

"I'm afraid you can trust him, nevertheless. I've found it so myself. So tell him your business here and leave it to him as to what he puts in his paper."

Shannon headed a faction in the Pendergast organization. He was an independent old fellow, and he wasn't under Pendergast's thumb. Pendergast realized Shannon's power and the size of his following, so he and Shannon talked more as equals than as boss and bossee. On that footing Shannon had a degree of veto power over Pendergast's plans when they didn't please him.

Such was the situation in Missouri as I saw it through Joe Shannon's eyes in 1932. In that year Champ Clark's brilliant son, Bennett, was elected Senator.

Pendergast didn't want Bennett Clark to have that job; Bennett was high-spirited, of aristocratic background, not given to taking orders from bosses and, as Pendergast saw him, a hard man to control. Whether Pendergast liked the idea or not made little difference to Clark; he went after the nomination with the backing of powerful friends and won it, trouncing Pendergast in the primary election. Thereafter Clark and Pendergast made peace and Pendergast supported him in the general election.

Clark's good friend, Senator Harry B. Hawes, whom Clark was to succeed, thereupon did a fine and generous thing in Clark's behalf. He resigned from the Senate, permitting Clark to occupy the seat early in 1933, a month ahead of other Democratic senators elected in 1932. This move gave Clark seniority over all other Democrats elected for the first time to the Senate that year.

Clark's election was in the Missouri tradition. One of the senators was to come from the eastern part of the state, the other from the western part. When Clark took his seat, Missouri's other senator was a Republican, Roscoe C. Patterson of Kansas City. Patterson then had two more years to serve. It was recognized tacitly that Patterson's successor should come from western Missouri. There the Pendergast organization was dominant; and it was generally understood that Pendergast would name the candidate.

When the off-year campaign of 1934 approached, the New Deal tide was nearing its flood. Roosevelt was immensely popular and it was apparent to most of Missouri's politicians—Shannon being an exception—that Patterson's days in the Senate were numbered and that a Democrat would succeed him.

What Democrat?

Pendergast's first choice was James A. Reed of Kansas City. Reed, acid-tongued orator and flaming individualist, had been Senator when Wilson was President. Neither liked anything about the other. Reed's term ended when the Harding avalanche swept the country in 1920. In 1934 he was living in retirement and old age was creeping toward him. But he still retained much of his early fire and vigor.

Pendergast turned to Shannon and asked what he thought about Reed as the nominee.

"Jim Reed is an able man," Shannon told him. "And one of the most difficult; I've heard that he can't even get along with himself at times. He's a good vote-getter and I think he could win, if any Democrat could. But he's getting old. And he's comfortable. I don't think he'll run."

Reed didn't run. What happened between him and Pendergast was made some sort of mystery; Shannon never told me the details. All I could get him to say after the decision had been made, was "Reed isn't going to run."

And then Shannon delighted and annoyed me with one of those confidences a newsman loves and hates at the same time—loves it because it gives him an inside view of what's going on and hates it because he can't print it.

"Pendergast has asked me to take the nomination for Senator," Shannon said. "What do you think of that, Brother Helm?"

"I think you'd make a good senator," I replied. "That is, as good a senator as any Jeffersonian Democrat could make of himself under the New Deal."

"That's the hell of it," he said warmly. "This man Roosevelt—only the Lord knows where he's leading the country. He's no more a Jeffersonian Democrat than a jackrabbit. But he's got the Jeffersonian Democrats, the real Democrats, hogtied. They've got to go along with him and his notions. They haven't anywhere else to go. They've got to support him because they haven't got anybody else to support."

That was different music from a box that publicly played the prevailingly popular Roosevelt praises. But it came, I knew, from Joe Shannon's heart; and it was mild and pleasant when compared with what I was to hear during the remaining years of Shannon's dozen in Congress.

I recall the solemnity with which he spoke. He had taken my arm and guided me out of his office and into the corridor. We stood opposite his doorway at a window overlooking the inner court of the New House Office Building. Although we were alone he lowered his voice to a whisper.

"I fear," he whispered slowly and emphatically, "that Roosevelt and his clan are trying to set up a dynasty in this country. The King, the Queen and Crown Prince Jimmy. They have fastened themselves on the Democratic party with a new and strange philosophy; they're undoing all the good the Democratic party has done in a century when it followed the principles of Thomas Jefferson."

Was he going to run? I asked.

Well, he didn't know. He hadn't made up his mind; he wanted to think it over. Pendergast was pressing him to take it and get busy, but he was going to take his time to decide. He wanted to talk it over with some of his friends back home, including Frank Walsh, and size the situation up.

I tried to get his permission to write a story for the *Journal-Post* under my by-line and without committing him in any way. I wanted to scoop the *Star* again. He seemed to resent even the suggestion as he turned, almost savagely, and looked straight into my eyes.

"Write nothing," he said impatiently. "You know I would not have brought you out here and told you this if I thought you were going to use it for a story. Keep it to yourself."

From that day to this, I have done so. Now the story is more than a dozen years old and Joe Shannon has been gathered to his fathers. Were he living I feel he would give me the permission he denied me then.

"Who'll run for senator if you don't?" I asked. "Who has Pendergast in mind that could take the place if you turned it down?"

Never mind about that, he told me, still jolted by my desire to rush into print with his secret. There would be a man to take it, never fear, and we would cross that bridge when we came to it.

As I left him I felt sure he wouldn't take the nomination.

Apart from his age, there were good reasons why he wouldn't. As a member of the House, he was reasonably secure and probably could come back to Washington as long as he wanted. He had made a name in his four years in Congress. A year or so earlier he had headed a special House committee to investigate his hobby, government competition with private business. He was liked by his colleagues. And he had a strong and rapidly increasing dislike for Franklin Roosevelt, head of his party, even then. Jefferson, Roosevelt's antithesis, was his idol.

Thus Pendergast's second choice for the senatorial nomination faded out as had the first. When Shannon definitely turned it down, I asked him again whom Pendergast had in mind.

"I don't know for certain," he replied, "but he's talking about Judge Truman."

"And who," I asked, "is Judge Truman?"

"He's Pendergast's third choice for the nomination."

"A lawyer?"

"No; he's not a lawyer. He gets his title of Judge because he is a member of what you might call our Jackson County board of commissioners. They run the county's affairs and they are called judges."

"Oh," I said, "just like lawyers in the South are called Colonels, I suppose."

"Exactly. It's a courtesy title."

"Well, what sort of judge is Mr. Truman?"

"A pretty good one," Shannon replied. "Yes, I'd say a pretty good one when it comes to running the county's business. I'll say to his credit that he's done a good job. And he's clean. Even the *Star* hasn't been able to dig up anything to his discredit that they could use against him."

"I never heard of him," I replied.

"That's the trouble, Brother Helm. Hardly anybody out-side of Jackson County knows him or of him. He's prac-tically unknown, and that isn't going to help the ticket."

"If obscurity is his only sin," I reminded Mr. Shannon, "it needn't be fatal, you know."

"Of course not. Not fatal; and it isn't helpful, either. Why, Harry Truman isn't known even out-State. We'd have to run a sort of educational campaign to let people know who he is."

"What do you think of him?"

"Well, I don't know. I think we ought to nominate a strong man, not an unknown. We're going to have a hard fight this fall to elect even a strong man, and I doubt if Truman's strong enough to pull through. And I'm certain he won't add any strength to the ticket as a whole. Roose-velt isn't running this year, you know, and the ticket has got to be elected on its own. People are going to look it over pretty carefully, I think."

He might be mistaken about that, he added. "Anyhow, it hasn't been settled yet."

Not long, however, was it to remain unsettled. A few days later when I dropped in at Shannon's office I found his secretary, Miss Arceneaux, worried and uncomfortable.

"I'm trying to get Mr. Shannon on the phone," she ex-plained. "He's off on one of his little trips making a speech against the government in business. I know where he is but I'm having trouble in reaching him. And I've got to reach him."

I didn't ask why and she didn't volunteer any further

information. Not long thereafter I learned that she had succeeded in getting him on the phone. He was at Wilmington, Delaware. She told him Pendergast had called from Kansas City; that Pendergast had practically decided to put Truman on the ticket.

"Get him back, Allthy," Shannon instructed, mispronouncing, as always, her pretty first name, Althea. "Tell him not to do anything more about it till he hears from me. I'll phone him later today."

Shannon hurriedly left his Wilmington party and headed for Washington. Late in the afternoon he bustled in to his office and made a beeline for the telephone.

"Don't tell the newspapers or anybody else," he telephoned to Pendergast. "Hold it up until I can talk it over with you. I'm taking the night train for Kansas City."

In a day or so the news was out. Truman was the man, and Shannon was back in Washington.

"Well," I greeted him, "I see you've named your candidate for Senator."

"Not my candidate," Shannon corrected. "Pendergast's. And now that it's done, it's done, and I'm going to work for the whole ticket."

"What do you think of the selection?"

"Not a hell of a lot."

"Why not, Mr. Shannon?"

"I'm afraid, as I told you before, that Truman's too light. He's a good mixer, a very pleasant sort of fellow. And he's clean. I suspect that was one of the chief reasons Tom wanted him. The *Star's* been hammering Tom hard and he naturally wants to make sure his man's all right.

"I haven't got anything against Truman; in fact, I like him. On the other hand, I haven't got much for him. He makes a fair speech without much punch in it, but he's apt to spoil his chances by his habit of dancing around nervously. Like this."

Shannon affected a grimacing grin, raised and lowered his arms rapidly like a rooster flapping its wings, and pattered around the floor in quick little jerky steps. I laughed. Coming out of his pantomime, Shannon laughed, too.

"It isn't quite as bad as that," he conceded, "but the fellow's always grinning and he's too quick with his mouth. He talks off the cuff at the wrong time; doesn't stop to consider what he's going to say before out pop the words. I don't think he's heavy enough for the Senate. I can't imagine him there and I doubt if he can be elected."

"Did you ask Pendergast not to name him?"

"No; I didn't go that strong. We talked it over and concluded Truman would be as good a bet as he could make. You know, Brother Helm, Tom hasn't got a field of world-beaters to pick from. I agreed to the choice."

Shannon's description of Truman was unkind and unjustified, I concluded after Truman had come to Washington. And Shannon himself changed his opinion later.

"I like the way he votes," Shannon told me toward the end of the first session of Truman's tenure as Senator. "He votes right. He shows he wants to do something for the poor devils that have been exploited. Between Capital and Labor, you know just where to find him all the time. You'll find him the champion of the little man, never of the plutocrats."

So completely did Shannon revise his earlier estimate that when Truman ran for re-election in 1940, Shannon worked enthusiastically for his success.

There was an unusual sequel to Shannon's somewhat reluctant approval of Truman in 1934.

Shannon was becoming old and infirm after serving twelve years in the House, and in 1942 he decided not to run again. Roger C. Slaughter succeeded him in January, 1943. And Slaughter was defeated for renomination in 1946 because of the opposition of Harry Truman. Pendergast was dead and his nephew, James Pendergast, headed the Democratic organization in Kansas City.

Truman opposed Slaughter because, as a member of the House Committee on Rules, Slaughter had voted in this key committee to block legislation Truman advocated. Jim Pendergast sided with Truman, and the organization swung in behind the man of Truman's choice, Enos Axtell, Slaughter's opponent in the primary. Axtell won the nomination. In the general election, however, Axtell was defeated. For the first time in many years Shannon's old district was represented in Congress by a Republican.

One of the breaks that helped Truman on his way to the White House occurred when he was only twenty-eight years old.

This was spawned in the heat and turmoil of the Democratic National Convention at Baltimore in 1912. Truman was a thousand miles away and had nothing whatever to do with it. He probably witnessed it from afar with lively interest, though he didn't dream at the time that it would ever affect him personally. Indeed, I doubt if he linked the event later with his rise in politics—I have never discussed it with him—but beyond question it played a part in piloting him to the Presidency.

I had a newsman's inside view of what was going on at that time and recall it as vividly as if it occurred last week.

The *Associated Press* had assigned me a few weeks before to cover Governor Woodrow Wilson at Sea Girt, N. J., the summer home provided by the state for its Chief Executive. When the balloting at Baltimore got under way Wilson made a poor start. Champ Clark of Missouri, Speaker of the House, got off to an early lead. Clark was supported by William Jennings Bryan and his following.

In those days the Democratic party's rules required a two-thirds vote to nominate its candidates for President and Vice President. In 1912 in Republican ranks there was a split between Theodore Roosevelt and President William Howard Taft. Because of this split it was virtually a cinch that the Democratic nominee would win the election.

For several days the Baltimore Convention was in deadlock because of the two-thirds rule. On the lawn of the Sea Girt mansion, a tent had been set up and a telegraph line had been run to the tent for the convenience of the dozen or more newsmen with Wilson. Jack Mendelson, an oldtime Morse press operator, was in charge.

The torrid season was at its height in Baltimore when the Convention met and some of the sessions were held at night. As the ballots were taken, Mendelson received reports over his wire. These he would pass among the newsmen and show to Wilson or his secretaries, Joe Tumulty and Walter Measday.

I remember well the night Clark reached the peak of his

strength. He then had more than a majority of the votes but was short of the required two-thirds. We all sat in chairs on the lawn, in a rough semi-circle in the light from Mendelson's tent. It was chilly and blankets had been sent over from the armory near by.

Woodrow Wilson was in the center of the half-moon line. He had a blanket draped carelessly over his shoulders. In the mansion whose windows were bright with light waited Mrs. Wilson and the three Wilson girls, Margaret, Eleanor, and Jessie.

As reports of the balloting were received Mendelson would dash out from his tent and read the results so all could hear. Wilson made no comments as to these. For more than two hours he stayed with us, the life of the party with amusing anecdotes and limericks some of which he had composed himself. He was gay and debonair at his darkest hour; what was going on at Baltimore he seemed to regard as impersonally as the man in the moon.

How Bryan deserted Clark and swung to Wilson; how Wilson soon thereafter was nominated, are well known political history.

A few days later, a hundred or so Democratic members of the House came by special train from Washington to Sea Girt to meet Wilson and congratulate him. Brave old Champ Clark, the loser, led the delegation. With Clark was his son, Bennett, a young man who even then had started on a promising political career. I met him there for the first time. I think he was Parliamentarian of the House at that time, although he probably was no more than twenty-five years of age.

Bennett Clark never forgave Bryan for deserting his father and switching his support to Wilson. But for Bryan's desertion, Champ Clark probably would have been the nominee and would have been elected President.

The two-thirds rule that contributed to Champ Clark's defeat also rankled in Bennett's bitter memories. Under that rule delegates from the Southern States—which since the day of Grover Cleveland had been the only consistently Democratic part of the country and had contributed the great majority of Democratic votes in the Electoral College—had virtual veto power over the nomination. They numbered always more than one-third of the total; by uniting in opposition to any candidate they could defeat him.

Bennett Clark wanted that rule set aside. His big chance to have this done came in 1936 when the nominating Convention was held at Philadelphia. Missouri's delegation was headed by Bennett, then the state's senior senator. The junior senator, Harry Truman, also was a delegate. Congress had adjourned the night before the Convention opened, and Truman picked up his secretary, Victor Messall, and myself the next day, and drove up in his car.

Incidentally, Truman's driving was of the get-there-soon variety, and I'll never forget that ride with him at the wheel.

Franklin Roosevelt, nearing the end of his first term, was unopposed for the nomination. After he had been nominated, Clark offered a resolution to end the time-honored, two-thirds rule. The Convention adopted it— and the veto power of the South thereupon was ended.

Under the new procedure, only a simple majority of the delegates' votes was required to nominate, as was the rule at Republican conventions.

There, at long last, Bennett Clark rubbed from the rule book the words that had barred his father from the White House nearly a generation before. In doing so, he brought about a situation that was to aid in nominating Truman for the Vice Presidency in 1944, although neither he nor Truman thought so at the time.

Repeal of that rule in 1936 contributed to the nomination of Roosevelt for a third term in 1940 and a fourth term in 1944.

In both of those years there was strong opposition in the party to violating the two-term precedent established by George Washington. This opposition was vocalized by Jim Farley, the National Committee Chairman who managed Roosevelt's first and second Presidential election campaigns. Opposition was strongest in the traditionally conservative South. Powerful party leaders from the South had wearied of the New Deal and its presiding genius.

But in 1940 and 1944 the South had lost its veto power. The two-thirds rule had been repealed. Southern leaders had no place to go other than the New Deal camp. Even such an outstanding leader as Walter George of Georgia whom Roosevelt had tried in vain to purge from the Senate in 1938 had to rally around Roosevelt or rally not at all. They made the best of the distasteful circumstances, publicly supporting Roosevelt; privately they were sullen and rebellious.

Under the old rule, they would have had a chance, by uniting, to form a tight bloc of one-third or more of the delegates and thus defeat the Roosevelt machine. They stood no chance of doing this when a majority of the delegates was necessary to their success.

The uncaptained opposition got nowhere. Repeal of the two-thirds rule championed in 1936 by Bennett Clark throttled any such plans they may have entertained. The way now was wide open for Roosevelt to arrange for his own draft and to name his running mate, Harry Truman.

This turn of the political wheel produced its own little ironies. In 1944, Bennett Clark went down to defeat in his fight for re-election to the Senate. The election that sent Harry Truman's star to its zenith, sent Bennett Clark's to its nadir.

Chapter Three

———✳———

LIKE many another congressional freshman, Harry Truman learned early in his Washington service that there is more than one kind of newspaperman.

One kind—the largest group—is the reporter. He reports what is said and done, doesn't fight the news or quarrel with it. He may agree with everything a politician says or he may not believe a word of it. It makes no difference; if he is a good reporter he sends an accurate story to his newspaper, uncolored by his personal views.

Many Washington reporters write under their names, or by-lines. In that case, the reporter has more leeway for then not only may he report what's going on but he may attempt to interpret the news. By-line reporters as a rule go to great pains to be fair and to present both sides of a question, particularly if it should be highly controversial.

Such newspapermen make up the great majority of the capital's correspondents. With these Harry Truman had no quarrel.

Another kind of Washington newspaperman is the columnist. Generally he has been a working reporter. He signs his stuff and slants it toward his own viewpoint or the bent of the editors who employ him or buy his writings. Sometimes he is a specialist writing on a few broad subjects of which he has a first rate personal knowledge. He writes opinion largely, editorials rather than straight news.

Correspondents of that sort usually are hard-working fellows with a flair for turning a happy phrase. Because they generally are fair and unprejudiced, Truman does not feel he has suffered at their hands, with one or two notable exceptions.

A third kind of newspaperman is the pundit. He signs his contributions and takes himself very seriously, giving an impression at times that he is a statesman in disguise. Some of these writers who have been high in official life are really not newspapermen at all; they are has-beens making money out of the fact that once they were prominent.

A pundit columnist is never hampered by the facts. When he meets a fact he doesn't like, he can do one of several things. He can ignore it. He can soft-pedal it, play it down below its true perspective and thus minimize it. Or he can wring its little neck, distort its little body and shape it into a grotesque something no whit resembling its original form.

Such writers are apt to develop into public scolds and as a rule don't last long in the writing business. Because their readers soon learn they are phonies, they are here today and gone tomorrow.

Truman feels he has been misrepresented grossly many

times by that sort of newspaperman. He has felt so from the beginning of his stay in Washington.

In my own daily contacts with Truman, I aimed at being a good by-line reporter and never a pundit. Readers of the Kansas City *Journal-Post*, I felt, were much more interested in what he said and did than in what I thought of what he said and did. Nevertheless, I pondered many a time over one strange fact in Harry Truman's political life. That was his fondness for and complete loyalty to Tom Pendergast, Missouri's Democratic boss.

They were so utterly different in every way, yet Truman came to Washington thinking Pendergast the salt of the earth. Usually when black and white mix the result is gray; yet here black remained black and white remained white. It seemed incredible, yet I had almost daily evidence of its truth.

"Don't let the *Star* crowd get you down on Pendergast, Bill," Truman told me early in his Senate days. "He isn't what they say he is. I know."

Harry Truman was my good and helpful friend, a square shooter and incorruptible, and I took his word for it. For more than three years I rated the Pendergast I had never seen not as a crooked politician but as an able leader vilified by disgruntled writers on my opposition paper. In that period I saw Pendergast wholly through Truman's eyes. Yet even on that basis I could not explain fully to myself the persistence and vigor of the attacks upon him.

"Why doesn't Pendergast show those fellows up?" I asked.

"I don't know," Truman replied. "I think he ought to. But Tom just doesn't pay any attention to them."

[42]

Many times I asked if Pendergast were really on the level.

Always the answer from Truman was an emphatic Yes. He had yet to learn of a single discreditable thing Pendergast had ever done, he assured me. I believed it then and I believe it now—as of that time. On the contrary, Truman told me, Pendergast had helped make Kansas City; he had found the place a struggling town and had contributed toward making it a great city.

"Then he surely must resent the attacks that are made on him," I persisted.

"Certainly he does," Truman said, "but he never replies to them."

"I am wondering if he wouldn't like to be presented in his true light to the public.

Truman wanted to know how that could be done.

There were a lot of ways, I told him. One way would be for a trained writer to present the truth in a biography of Pendergast. Such a book, I added, could be written if Pendergast were willing to cooperate.

"I think that's a good suggestion," Truman said, "but I doubt if he would agree to it."

Why not? I wanted to know.

Truman said he knew Pendergast well from long association and that Pendergast had an extreme dislike for publicity. I argued that if Pendergast resented the wrong sort of publicity he ought to be willing to cooperate in presenting the correct story of himself and his affairs; that he should welcome an opportunity to get the right sort of publicity. Moreover, I continued, Truman himself ought to be interested in having the truth published.

"The public thinks he's a hard-boiled political boss," I said, "and that you take orders from him."

"He has never tried to influence me in anything I've done except once," Truman replied, "and you know all about that."

"Besides putting your friend right with the public, I could make a lot of money if I wrote that book," I continued. "And now I'm thinking of Helm and not of Pendergast or Truman."

Truman laughed. "I thought so when you started the conversation," he said. "Do you want to write Tom's biography?"

"I certainly do, if he's on the level like you say he is."

"All right, Bill, I'll help you if I can. I think you've got a good suggestion and I'll put it up to Tom when I go back to Kansas City. But I don't think he'll agree."

I asked him to tell Pendergast I would get leave of absence from the *Journal-Post*, that I would come to Kansas City and get material for the book.

"At your own expense?" Truman asked.

"At my own expense," I repeated. "I'm willing to take the gamble. You say he's all right and that's good enough for me."

"I think such a book ought to be written," Truman said. "But I don't think it will be. I don't think Tom will relish the idea."

Pendergast didn't "relish the idea," Truman told me a few weeks later.

"I can't convince him," Truman said, "but maybe you can. If you want to take a shot at it I'll try to arrange it."

"How?"

"Well, he goes to Atlantic City usually in the summer. I think he'll be going there soon. I'll see him before he leaves Kansas City and try to make an appointment for you to discuss the matter with him in Atlantic City. I'll let you know."

By that time I was eager to write the book for which I imagined there would be a large demand. I thanked Truman and told him I thought I could convince Pendergast that the book should be written.

Truman's grin widened. "Good luck to you," he said.

"You'll find him a hard man to convince," he went on. "He's set in his ideas and I think you're riding for a fall. You'll find him a rough sort of fellow, but he'll treat you right. If he says he'll go along with the idea, you can depend on it. He never breaks a promise."

That was in the summer of 1938. I had not met Pendergast and knew him only by reputation. Not long thereafter Truman made a trip to Kansas City and early in August I received the following telegram from him:

"Pendergast at Hotel Traymore, Atlantic City, where he will see you. Wire him for appointment."

I telegraphed my thanks to Truman and sent a wire to Pendergast.

SENATOR TRUMAN WIRES ME YOUR WILLINGNESS TO GRANT ME AUDIENCE TO DISCUSS PUBLICATION I PROPOSED TO HIM WHICH I UNDERSTAND HE HAS TAKEN UP WITH YOU WOULD BE GRATEFUL IF YOU WOULD GIVE ME A FEW MINUTES AT YOUR CONVENIENCE SOON

[45]

Pendergast telegraphed me telling me to come along and I called on him at his hotel.

Truman was right; Pendergast was as tight as concrete in his refusal to have anything to do with the publication of his biography.

"So far as my friends are concerned," he said, "I don't have to have a book written about me. They know me. As for the people who don't know me, I don't give a damn. If they want to believe the lies printed about me, they can do so."

I accepted that, of course, as final. After seeing him for the first time, I felt relieved by the decision. Instead of being disappointed, I was happy. The moment I saw him I knew that even if he were as upright as a telephone pole he would be almost impossible as a collaborator.

"I didn't think he would go along," Truman commented when I told him the upshot of my Atlantic City excursion. "But you were so dead set on it, I thought I'd help you all I could. When Tom says he'll do something, he'll do it and you can bank on it. But when he says he won't, he won't— and you can bank on that, too."

It was about nine months later that Pendergast pleaded guilty to an indictment charging him with income tax evasion. Had the book been written it would have come from the press just about the time the Grand Jury handed up its true bill. And so, as it turned out, Pendergast did me a very great favor. Truman, too; for his name would have been found on many a page of the Pendergast biography and . . .

Once more the Providence that watches over Harry

Truman saved him from his friends and gave him the breaks.

When Pendergast went to court with a confession of guilt on his lips, Truman was hurt and astounded. I am sure he had little inkling of his old friend's troubles before the Grand Jury returned its indictment. Even then he seemed to cling to the hope that Pendergast somehow would prove his innocence, that here was the climactic political attack upon him in a long series of attacks.

Franklin Roosevelt knew, of course, of Pendergast's impending disgrace. So did Lloyd Stark, the Governor of Missouri, who was a frequent caller at the White House while Federal agents were weaving the net around Pendergast. Stark, like Truman, had come to high office with the stamp of Pendergast's approval upon him. That was in 1936, when Stark was elected Governor.

Bitterness developed between Stark and Pendergast not long after the election. And as it was Harry Truman's second nature to make his close friends' enemies his enemies, bitterness was not long in developing between Stark and Truman. This strong feeling resulted two years thereafter in as hot a political fight between them as Missouri had ever seen—and in Missouri no such fight is even warm until the boiling point is reached.

The immediate cause of the disagreement between Pendergast and Stark was the latter's refusal to continue a Pendergast henchman in office as State Insurance Commissioner. This henchman, it developed in court, had been associated with Pendergast in dealings involving certain funds impounded in a dispute between the state and a group of insurance companies. The deal ended the dispute and Pendergast received a large sum of money. It was his failure to report the money as income that led to his indictment.

When Pendergast and Stark were at the climax of their controversy, Truman was called on the long distance telephone by Pendergast. The call had nothing to do with the controversy. It carried a suggestion from Pendergast that Truman vote a certain way on a matter to come shortly before the Senate. Truman told me at the time—and subsequently on several occasions—that it was the only time Pendergast had tried to influence his vote.

Truman turned him down.

I understood from Truman then that the call had been made at the instance of Franklin Roosevelt. Truman apparently was under that impression at the time. Later he told me that he understood Pendergast had called him at Jim Farley's instigation. Farley then was Postmaster General and Chairman of the Democratic National Committee. If Farley instigated the call, I assume he did so after talking with Roosevelt.

The date of the call was July 19, 1937.

Pendergast was on a brief vacation at Colorado Springs. Stark had followed him there and on the day the call was made the two of them were wrangling over the Insurance commissionership. The controversy had become acrid. It was ironical that a request from Washington to Pendergast to influence Truman's vote was timed at a moment when he was steeped to his ears in serious trouble.

What Washington wanted of Pendergast—and whether Pendergast received the call from Roosevelt or Farley seems relatively unimportant as undoubtedly they had talked it over together—was quite simple. Pendergast was to get Truman to vote for Alben Barkley in his contest with Pat Harrison for the Majority leadership of the Senate.

Truman had promised his vote to Harrison, Senator from Mississippi and Chairman of the powerful Finance Committee. Roosevelt was pulling wires to bring about Barkley's election. The race was neck and neck, but a private poll of members taken by Farley indicated that Barkley would be defeated and that Harrison would win by a single vote.

What they had to do to put their man across was to switch one vote from the Harrison column to Barkley.

They decided that Truman was the man to switch.

Barkley supporters had solicited his vote without success. Thereupon Roosevelt and Farley, familiar with Truman's political background and apparently believing him amenable to orders from Pendergast, decided—one or both of them—to get Pendergast to persuade Truman to switch.

What inducement, if any, was offered Pendergast in this undertaking, I do not know. The incident was a good illustration, however, of machine politics as manipulated behind the scenes: Roosevelt appealing either directly or through his campaign manager to a political boss for a vote in the Senate!

Roosevelt had reasons for wanting Barkley elected Majority Leader. He had appraised the qualities of both Barkley and Harrison and concluded that he could go further in accomplishing New Deal objectives with Barkley carrying the banner. That was no reflection whatever on Barkley; rather it was a compliment on the President's part. It may have been a reflection on Harrison's ability as a New Deal leader but if it were so intended, nothing was said about it publicly.

. The time was a critical period in Roosevelt's career. Fresh from the sweeping victory of his second election campaign, Roosevelt a few months earlier had proposed packing the Supreme Court. His notion had resulted in a violent upheaval among his followers. It split the Democrats in both Houses and was the big issue before Congress at the time.

From the day of Roosevelt's first inauguration, Senator Robinson of Arkansas had been Majority Leader of the Senate. He had exerted himself in Roosevelt's behalf for more than four years as pilot of all New Deal legislation through the Senate. Now the vast stir and commotion over the court-packing proposal overtaxed his strength. He was stricken and died suddenly. His death created a vacancy in the key post essential to success of the Roosevelt proposal in the Senate.

After Robinson's death, Roosevelt took personal command of the deteriorating situation in the Senate. His first insurance, naturally, was to be that the new Majority Leader would fight well and intelligently for his policies. Barkley, he decided, was the man. He so advised Farley who beat the political tom-tom to summon the New Deal tribe to the Barkley camp.

The appeal to Pendergast to make Truman switch his support from Harrison to Barkley came by long distance telephone. Truman was under the impression after talking with Pendergast that the call to Pendergast came from the White House. A similar call was made to James Aylward, Chairman of the Missouri State Democratic Committee.

Aylward and Pendergast were relied on to make Truman change his mind and vote the way Roosevelt wanted him to vote.

When I saw him that morning, an hour or so after Pendergast had telephoned him, Truman was still agitated and a bit upset.

"You could never guess what happened to me," he greeted me. "Tom Pendergast phoned me and asked me to vote for Barkley for Majority Leader. And I had to turn him down.

"Jim Aylward phoned me, too. I didn't mind turning Jim down, not so much, anyhow, but to say No to Tom was one of the hardest things I ever had to do. It's the first time Tom asked me to do anything since I came to the Senate."

"What did he say?"

"He said he had got a telephone call from the White House asking him to try to get me to change over from Harrison to Barkley. He told 'em he would pass along the request, but that I was one of the most obstinate fellows he'd ever met and that he didn't think his request would be worth a damn if I'd made up my mind to vote for Harrison."

"Did you tell Pendergast you wouldn't vote for Barkley?"

"I did. There isn't any reason in the world why I shouldn't vote for Barkley except one. I like him and admire him and I honestly think he would make a good leader. The one reason why I can't vote for him is that I've promised my vote to Pat."

[51]

"Did you tell that to Pendergast?"

"I said, 'I just can't do it, Tom, and I'll tell you why. I've given my word to Pat Harrison. You know how that is, Tom; you know better than any other man in politics. When you give your word you keep it and everybody can count on your keeping it. That's the way it is with me.'

"And he said that it was all right, that it didn't make a helluva lot of difference to him but that the White House had called him and asked him to get me on the phone and that he had said he would do it. And that's all there was to it."

Truman kept his promise. He voted for Harrison. The White House found another New Deal senator willing to switch. Harrison lost by one vote and that vote wasn't Truman's. Barkley won and carried the New Deal flag through thick and thin for seven years. When he tried, in an angry moment in 1944, to pass it on to other hands Roosevelt publicly smoothed his ruffled feathers and persuaded him to stay on. He did so when Truman became President and until after the election of 1946 when the Republicans captured the Senate. Thereafter he became Minority Leader and continued to carry on for Truman.

I wonder: Did Harry Truman dream by any chance in July, 1937, when he voted against Barkley that within a few spinning years he would be calling on Barkley to carry his flag in the Senate? Did Alben Barkley have a vision that July day of the man whose vote all but cost him the post he coveted giving him orders from the White House?

Probably not.

Roosevelt's play to Pendergast annoyed Truman and to close friends he voiced his irritation—guardedly at first, then with increasing candor. Other irritations had preceded it and were to follow. As time passed, Truman's feeling became manifest to a widening circle. Finally he no longer concealed it and mentioned it even to casual friends.

"I'm tired of being pushed around," he told some of them, "tired of having the President treat me like an office boy."

It was inevitable that Roosevelt would get the echo of this. With characteristic directness and bluntness, Truman decided to let the President have the correct version. He telephoned the White House to make sure that Roosevelt would get the story straight. The President was not available and someone else—Stephen Early of the secretariat, Truman told me—took the message.

Truman told me of the call at the time.

He said he reminded the astonished Early that he (Truman) was a senator representing the State of Missouri. He added that he expected the consideration and courtesy to which his high office entitled him. And that, he continued, applied to everybody with whom he had official relationship, including the President of the United States. Would Mr. Early be so good as to convey that message to the President?

"What did Steve say when you told him that?" I asked.

"He said, 'Very well, Senator, I will.'"

Probably one reason why Truman felt he was being pushed around was rooted in the hot congressional fight over the courtpacking plan. Truman supported Roosevelt in this proposal, but Missouri's senior senator, Bennett Clark, did not. Clark opposed it vigorously and conspicuously; with Wheeler of Montana he led the opposition in the Senate. As punishment for such boldness, Roosevelt stripped Clark of all Federal patronage in Missouri. The White House let him know in definite and emphatic terms that the President would not care to receive from him any recommendation as to appointments to Federal office in the State of Missouri.

Next to retirement to private life, that is about the worst thing that could happen to any senator of the majority party.

Such patronage had been a senatorial prerogative for generations. Except for an occasional upset—as, for instance, when the man selected for a job was shown by investigation to be unfit for it or unworthy—a senator's recommendation to the President of his own party meant a nomination of the man recommended.

That applied to all political pap served in every state except postmasterships. Postmasters are "recommended" by representatives, one of the few crumbs of patronage a mere congressman gets from the White House. I know of the lovely theory that postmasters are appointed from the Civil Service list after taking a competitive examination; in case after case it just hasn't worked out that way—unless the candidate surviving the examination has his congressman's approval.

The extent of Federal patronage in Missouri was large. It was spreading toward its greatest dimensions when Clark was stripped of it. Appointees included not only officials of Federal courts, Federal Attorneys, Collectors of Internal Revenue and other regular jobholders; they included hundreds of appointments in the state to the numerous alphabetical agencies of the New Deal.

Through such patronage senators reward their supporters and keep their political machines in happy mind. A senator deprived of such patronage has a hungry machine on his hands back home. And political hunger is peculiarly bad; it sometimes results in a form of political cannibalism whereby the senator is eaten alive by his organization which thereupon proceeds to work for another candidate who presumably can command such patronage.

With Clark shorn of Missouri patronage, the natural assumption was that Clark's share would be diverted to Truman. It wasn't; not in full measure. Appointments were made in some cases without Truman's approval and in one outstanding case in direct opposition to his wishes.

Truman's feeling that he had been pushed around by the President came to its climax in 1938. In opposition to Truman's wishes, Maurice M. Milligan was nominated by Roosevelt for a second term as United States Attorney at Kansas City. Milligan had a brother in the House, "Tuck" Milligan, who was a personal friend of Clark. Early in his first term, Roosevelt had nominated Maurice Milligan to be United States Attorney on Clark's recommendation.

Maurice Milligan was Pendergast's arch-enemy. The reason why Pendergast hated him was that Milligan conducted the investigation that uncovered the malodorous vote frauds perpetrated by the Pendergast machine.

Pendergast's hatred of Milligan was sufficient reason for Truman to hate him, too. Milligan's second nomination to be United States Attorney was sent, unfortunately for Truman's peace of mind, to the Senate at a time when the prosecution of Pendergast's henchmen was rising to its zenith.

Truman saw red with both eyes when the nomination came up from the White House. He denounced it in probably the most vigorous address he ever made to the Senate. At that moment Truman seemed to totter on the brink of a complete break with Roosevelt.

"My opposition to Mr. Milligan began long before vote frauds were brought to light in Kansas City," Truman told his hushed colleagues. "His morals and political thinking never did appeal to me."

He read from a speech carefully prepared in advance.

"The President has appointed him," Truman continued, "and the President wants him confirmed because of a situation in Kansas City due to vote fraud prosecutions in the Federal Court. Mr. Milligan has been made a hero by the Kansas City *Star* and the St. Louis *Post-Dispatch* because of these prosecutions.

"The implication has been that any capable lawyer I would recommend for district attorney in western Missouri would not do his duty in regard to the vote fraud prosecutions. Every good lawyer and decent citizen in Jackson County is just as strongly opposed to vote frauds as the Kansas City *Star* and Mr. Milligan.

"The detail work and the actual trial of the vote fraud cases have all been done by Mr. Milligan's two able deputies and not by Mr. Milligan. If the district attorney's office was to have been rewarded for vote fraud prosecutions by a reappointment, one of these able deputies should have been appointed.

[56]

"Mr. Milligan has accepted emoluments in the form of fees in bankruptcy proceedings in the Federal Court of western Missouri. In fact, he has received more money in fees in one case than his salary has been from the Federal Treasury for a whole year.

"The Federal Court at Kansas City is presided over by two as violently partisan judges as have ever sat on a Federal bench since the Federalist judges of Jefferson's Administration. They are Merrill E. Otis and Albert L. Reeves. Mr. Reeves was appointed by that great advocate of clean, nonpartisan government, Warren G. Harding, and Mr. Otis was named by that other great progressive nonpartisan, Calvin Coolidge.

"These two judges have made it perfectly plain to Mr. Milligan—and he has been able to see eye to eye with them, due to the bankruptcy emoluments—that convictions of Democrats are what they want. Lawyers in Kansas City have been afraid to act as defendant attorneys in these cases because it was intimated plainly to them that the Federal Judges did not consider it the proper thing to do. Lawyers all expect to practice in the Federal Court. In fact, a good friend of mine told me that he didn't dare to act as a defendant attorney in these cases because he had important matters pending in Otis' court.

"No one in Jackson County is allowed on these jury panels. Everyone in a community of 600,000 people is barred from jury service in the Federal Court in western Missouri in these cases. Grand juries were handpicked and the attitude of the grand jurymen was ascertained by the court in advance.

"Petit jury panels are investigated by the Secret Service,

and if a man is found to have acquaintances in Jackson County he is barred from service.

"I say this to the Senate, Mr. President, that a Jackson County, Missouri, Democrat has as much chance of a fair trial in the Federal District Court of western Missouri as a Jew would have in a Hitler court, or a Trotsky follower before Stalin. . . .

"The President has made this a personal appointment at the behest of a rabidly partisan press, and I am saying that the approval of this district attorney is an approval of the Hitler-Stalin tactics pursued by the District Court in western Missouri.

"Because the President asked for him, I have not attempted to exercise the usual senatorial prerogative to block his confirmation. I think, however, I would not be doing my public duty if I did not tell the Senate just what he is doing."

The Senate promptly confirmed the nomination; not only in 1938 (Truman's address was delivered February 15 of that year) but again in 1942. Three times was Milligan nominated and three times confirmed.

He was not given a fourth nomination.

In 1945, when his third term ended, Harry Truman no longer was a member of the Senate. He was President.

"Three times are more than any man should be nominated as district attorney," he said.

Truman named another man for the office, Sam Wear, a personal friend who had helped in his primary campaign in 1940. Mr Wear was confirmed and Mr. Milligan was retired to private life.

Chapter Four

———————✳———————

I WAS prowling a second-floor corridor of the Capitol one afternoon when Harry Truman overtook me and grasped my arm. He had just had a new experience, he said, and wanted to tell me about it.

We stood aside opposite the door to the Secretary's office. Truman was in high spirits. It was the day before Franklin Roosevelt was sworn in as President for the fourth time and a vanguard of inaugural visitors were trooping through the Capitol. Truman had resigned that morning from the Senate and was to take the oath as Vice President the next noon.

"I met Downey over in the Office Building this morning," Truman said. He was referring to California's New Deal Senator. "Downey stopped me and looked at me severely. 'Have you resigned from the Senate?' he asked me.

" 'Yes, I have; I did so just now,' I told him.

" 'Are you certain about that?'

" 'Positive,' I said.

" 'Then come with me,' he told me. 'And walk behind me.'

"I'd never seen Downey that way before and it puzzled me. But I went along, a few steps behind him. He led me to his office, opened the door and went in first. I followed. We went to his inner office. He closed the door behind us.

" 'You are no longer a Senator, are you?' he asked.

" 'That's right,' I said.

" 'And you're not on the public pay roll at all?'

" 'No.'

" 'Just a plain mister without a job?'

" 'That's all.'

" 'Then I want to talk to you. Sit down over there next to the wall. Take that stiff, uncomfortable chair.'

"I sat where he told me. He went over to his own soft, padded chair at his desk, took his seat and began fumbling with some papers. Presently he looked up.

" 'Well, Mr. Truman, what can I do for you?' he asked."

With such horseplay Harry Truman left the Senate. His departure was ten years, almost to the day, from the time he entered it.

The Senate into which the eager Truman was projected in January, 1935, was made up largely of contradictions and paradoxes. It still is. It is at once the most clannish of clubs or the stuffiest, according to the viewpoint. A likable, good-natured member like Truman can find fun galore in his work; a spirit of teasing runs through its grilling toil like lean meat in a bacon rasher. On the other hand, the Senate has an alchemy all its own; it can change a genial human being into an arrogant tub of self-importance in less than a forty-hour week. Occasionally it does so.

Nor can all the prophets of the world forecast what the Senate will do for a new member. That depends almost entirely on his own proclivities. If he lacks a sense of humor, he's sunk when he makes the plunge. A solemn man with a stuffed-shirt complex is likely to be overwhelmed by delusions of his own greatness. A good mixer with a line of horse sense will become a better mixer with more horse sense. His usefulness will expand while his hatband doesn't.

Exquisite, painful formality is of the essence of the Senate air. Common civility is distorted, at times, into princely foolishness. The senator from Florida for instance, must be referred to as the "gentleman from Florida" even when he is likened unfavorably to a skunk as he was not long ago.

In debate every senator is addressed by every other senator with words a commoner would use to salute a superman. "My distinguished friend for whom I entertain profound regard and the highest affection" dots the daily journal. "The able and learned Senator" from So-and-so is a close second.

The distinguished friend may be no more distinguished than a one-eyed potato and much less useful, and the "able and learned" senator may be a notorious wind-jamming bore that empties the galleries, but it's all the same in debate. Nobody even smiles at the joke. Every member's pan stays dead. It is not regarded as a joke; it's deeply serious stuff, and no fooling.

Courtesy comes in comic chunks. A member may detach another member's hide and nail it to the barn door, and that's quite all right if the job is done courteously. No such tenderness or deference attaches to non-members, however. They are not referred to as able, learned, distinguished, or objects of profound affection. Knowing that he cannot be sued for anything he says in the Senate Chamber, a senator denouncing a mere taxpayer can really go to town.

Each senator possesses a bushel or so of what he calls his prerogatives. These start with priority on Capitol elevators —a senator's three rings will stop a car anywhere in its shaft and swing it quickly to him—and extend to his privilege of blocking confirmation of a presidential nominee on the ground that the nominee is "personally objectionable" to the member. They run the range from Apollinaris Water to senility. The closer a majority party senator is to his second childhood, the greater his importance; the longer he has been in the Senate the more attenuated his seniority and the greater his honors. The oldest denizens get the most plush.

Freshmen senators are expected to be seen but never to be heard except to vote right. Such is the unwritten rule. As a consequence, the vigor and fresh blood of younger men must curdle in silence on the floor for at least the better part of their first session and preferably longer. The old boys are supposed to do all the talking.

Sometimes new members rebel. Truman was holding a whispered confab on the Senate floor one day with Senator McNary of Oregon, then the Minority Leader. A Republican senator was making a long-winded speech.

"He's a great trial to me," McNary confided, lolling back in his chair. "He talks too much and too soon."

The windbag finished almost before McNary had said it.

Another Republican who had been in the Senate less than a month but who already had made one long, tiresome speech, was recognized and started on a second.

"Well, what do you think of that fellow?" Truman asked with a grin.

"I'd say he was my No. 2 ————," McNary replied.

The tendency of some members is to strut and become pompous in a short time. Most of them, however, retain their perspective. After long exposure to Senatisis they are still good fellows, unspoiled.

Truman was of that group.

Probably nine times out of ten, new members come to the Senate full of pep and high purpose. Soon after taking the oath, a new member, unaccustomed to his surroundings, is apt to become unduly aware of the awful solemnity of his status; this after noting the owlish dignity of some of his seniors. The new member finds that the Senate has strict rules, regulations, and ropes none of which he may brush against without penalty. This realization comes to him all of a sudden. To find his way around he must learn the ropes like any first-grader in elementary school.

His reaction in a short time may be, "Migawd, I'm a member of the great United States Senate! I've got to act up to it."

And if he tries to do so, chances are he'll make an ass of himself.

Into this atmosphere went Harry Truman on January 3, 1935.

It was laden with perfume he had never breathed before and he came in meekly, somewhat awed and somewhat uncertain. In his own words he was "ignorant as a fool" of the Senate and its affairs. All he wanted—and he wanted that with feverish intensity and earnestness—was a chance to serve humbly. Wrapped in the hoary ritual of mid-Victorian humbuggery, it was given to him. He had the good sense to discard the wrapping.

Truman was one of a dozen freshmen senators sworn in from the Democratic side that day. Only one of that dozen remained in the 80th Congress, and he wasn't allowed to take his seat. The last survivor was Bilbo.

I talked with Truman the neophyte the day he took the oath of office. The grin that had captivated me when first I met him was gone. He stood now at the Senate's threshold, serious and a bit subdued as if he had glimpsed down a vista the staggering responsibilities of years to come. The humility he always wore still clothed him; he wore it that day with greater grace and charm.

It is my deep regret that I have no notes now of what he told me then. But I remember well the burden of his thoughts. Imperfectly, but in its essence, I give it as I now recall it.

"It is a high honor, but a still higher responsibility, to become a Senator of the United States and to be given a voice and a vote in the country's chief law-making body. I realize this today in its full measure, more than I have ever realized it before.

"I shall try to perform my duties to the best of my ability. In this I shall need the help and the prayers of those who have given me the privilege of serving them. For myself, I seek nothing from this service. My steadfast hope is that I may be given wisdom to perform my duties acceptably to those whom I want to serve."

This, in substance, he said without affectation and patently from his heart. In solemn mood, he talked with me of those whom Joe Shannon sometimes called the little people. He did not refer to them as the "little people," for that was not his phrase. The times were hard and the little people were suffering. Breadlines that had snaked in misery the length and breadth of the country were vivid memories of the recent past. They had been replaced to large extent by relief workers hired by New Deal agencies with public funds. But suffering still was acute and the lot of men and women who lived solely from labor was a hard lot.

Of this he talked with deep feeling. He hoped, he said, he would know what to do to help create conditions to improve their lot. A firmly fixed notion was in his mind that the little people had been exploited deliberately and ruthlessly by cliques of financial overlords. He wanted to do something about that, he said. In the years of his senatorship he was to voice this belief again and again, always with scorn and biting contempt for those he called Wall Street bankers and their allies.

In Harry Truman's heart, I knew then, was a deep reverence for God. I do not recall that he voiced it in that long talk or thereafter, but the inference was inescapable. He believed, I think, in the substance of religion rather than its ceremonial forms—and yet he was high in the rolls of Masonry. He lived cleanly and was honorable in his relations with his fellowmen.

By that rule, I thought, he had lived and would continue to live. In ways little and big he confirmed my belief. Truman had brought to the capital a heritage of debt from a period when he had been unsuccessful in business. These debts he paid with money scrimped from his public pay. It took years for him to settle the score; his wife performed their household chores herself to help him do so. To her he was always tenderly deferential whenever her name was brought into a conversation. The romance of his courtship had not altogether faded.

"She is the only sweetheart I ever had," he told me often.

Nor was he niggardly or parsimonious. I recall mentioning casually one day that I had not received my pay check and that it was overdue. It probably had been delayed by Jim Farley's bum postal service, I said. Vic Messall, Truman's secretary, was giving us a lift downtown from the Capitol in his car. To my astonishment, Truman had his wallet in his hand at once.

"I can lend you fifty, Bill, if that will help," he said.

I didn't take his fifty or any part of it and was in momentary embarrassment to explain that I wasn't hinting for a loan. Truman laughed heartily.

"I thought you were, you old black Republican," he teased. "It sounded that way to me. Didn't it sound that way to you, Vic?"

"It sure did," echoed Vic, a capable tease on his own account. "As a matter of fact, Senator, I thought he was going to ask you for it."

"It was perfectly plain to me that he had it in mind," Truman laughed, putting his wallet away. "Only don't hint next time, Bill. You don't have to hint. Just come out like a man and ask for it."

He shoved his thumb into my ribs and went off into a series of chuckles.

I know of only one resolution he made when he became a senator. He determined to master fully the details of legislation referred to his committees. He had only two ideas as to the committees on which he would prefer to serve.

In those days every freshman senator was assigned to two outstanding committees and to several minor ones. Truman's first interest was the Army; his second, transportation. These pointed him for membership in the Military Affairs and the Interstate Commerce Committees. He was named to the latter one when he entered the Senate but failed to get on the other for several years.

That was no reflection on him. Membership in the Military Affairs Committee was a prize plum. Alphabetically Truman was far down in the list of new senators and simply wasn't reached.

I learned of his committee preferences the first time I met him. We had talked only a few minutes when he told me that Eddie Meisburger, city editor of the *Journal-Post*, had served overseas with him in the First World War. He said Eddie was "a fine fellow," and had been "a good soldier." All the men in his company had been good soldiers, he added with his next breath. Truman had been captain of an artillery company which had seen service in France.

Of his old command he talked lovingly and often. It was, he thought, the finest group of men anywhere in the world. The war's end was more than sixteen years gone by as he talked, but he had kept in touch with his men, or many of them, during that period. His affection for them apparently heightened with the passing of time.

"We were together under fire," he said in a tone indicating there could hardly be a stronger tie among men, "and they behaved magnificently."

The great adventure of the First World War grooved Truman's interest to military affairs and bound him almost passionately to the Army. It stirred his active mind to inquiry and its tentacles reached out for the whys of military science. He became an eager student of strategy and tactics.

"Let me drive you up to Gettysburg some day soon," he suggested one morning. "We'll go over the battlefield and study the moves. I'll show you where your kinsman, Pickett, rocked the Union with his charge. I've been over that field myself, and you ought to know what happened there."

The invitation was repeated, but somehow the trip was never made. I wish it had been.

Truman's devotion to the Army did not blind him to its faults. Later in his official duties he was called on to put its High Command under the microscope and look for its flaws. When he found them, love of country soared above love of Army and he cracked down hard.

How his interest in transportation was aroused, I don't know but I suspect the wrecking of the Missouri Pacific railroad had much to do with it. This great carrier had been driven into bankruptcy. Manipulations of hungry bankers in New York City, he thought, were a primary cause. Part of the line's right of way lay through his state; he had been given a birdseye picture of the System's fraying. About that he was somewhat bitter and soon after his assignment to the Interstate Commerce Committee he bared the facts leading to the MoPac's troubles in an investigation remembered even today by those concerned.

Truman didn't place at once on the Military Affairs Committee, but he was assigned at the outset to the important Committee on Appropriations. Instead of having "something to do with the Army," as he wished, he was to have a great deal to do with public funds.

In Democratic rank on each of his main committees, he was last—fourteenth on Interstate Commerce, sixteenth on Appropriations. His other assignments were to the committees on Printing and Public Buildings and Grounds. On the first of these he stood fifth of the five Democratic members; on the second, eighth of the nine.

Only delay in filling the Public Buildings roster saved him from being the tail-ender Democrat on every committee to which he was assigned.

In the Senate Chamber, he was given a desk in the last row. In the Office Building, his suite consisted of three rooms on the second floor. They looked out on the grass-covered inner court.

He kept this suite, No. 240, until he moved to the White House. It was a sentimental attachment of a man given to sentiment. Here he had started his work and here he would finish it. After his inauguration as Vice President he was urged to move to the more pretentious quarters set aside for the Senate's presiding officer. He didn't want to go. His pretext for clinging to his old rooms was, "It's too much trouble to move."

Of the eleven new Democratic senators sworn in with freshman Truman, two became his warm friends. These were Lewis Schwellenbach of Washington and Sherman (Shay) Minton of Indiana. Both were Left-wing New Dealers. Truman himself was a New Dealer but no radical. My impression in those days was that he was a strong Party man following his leader with little questioning, although I felt that he doubted at times the wisdom of some of the policies he supported. Rarely was he off the reservation on a roll-call vote.

Truman was so fond of Schwellenbach that he wanted him near after becoming President and made him a member of the Cabinet in 1945. Of Minton, Truman saw little after 1940; Minton failed of re-election that year and later was made a Federal judge by Roosevelt.

With two junior senators who had preceded him by a year, Truman became very friendly. They were Hatch of New Mexico and O'Mahoney of Wyoming. Both were Left-wingers.

Politically, four of the new senators who took the oath when Truman did stood to his Right and four stood to his Left. Truman became intimate with none in either group. The first was comprised of Bilbo of Mississippi, Donahey of Ohio, Burke of Nebraska, and Gerry of Rhode Island, the last-named rated as one of the Senate's wealthiest members. The four to Truman's Left were Maloney of Connecticut, Holt of West Virginia, Moore of New Jersey, and Guffey of Pennsylvania.

Radcliffe of Maryland also was a newcomer in 1935.

At that period of free spending, membership on the Appropriations Committee was highly desired. To Truman, however, the assignment meant mainly additional work which he did not especially relish. Finance was not his strong point; indeed, it was one of his weakest.

The two-year-old New Deal Administration then was pump-priming and relieving, pouring out billions of public funds under both headings. A senator on the committee which channeled the big money was hailed as tops by the customers on whom he waited. Downtown there was a flourishing bureaucracy engaged in spending the billions he helped pilot to them; and this bureaucracy was alert to meet the wishes of such a senator. His opportunities for small-fry patronage were enormous.

Some of the committeemen fixed up their constituents with jobs all through the New Deal agencies; one, in particular, put thousands of his followers on the public pay rolls. But not Truman. There was more than a drop of Scotch blood in his veins to flare into private rebellion against boon-doggling. This blood was not so potent as to overcome his sense of Party loyalty. And if he held his nose on occasion when he passed the gravy, he held it in the privacy of the committee room where the ladle lay. He was not the man to start a public rumpus.

His heart wasn't wrapped up in the money-spending business, but he performed his committee work patiently and well. He doubtless would have been happier doing something other than to help shoot the national debt into the stratosphere. On rare occasions he spoke his mind about this, generally over a highball in his office. The money-spending policy was not of his making; it had been established by a higher authority and Truman's part in its play was that of a cog in the Party machinery.

To casual acquaintances Truman appeared an easy-going fellow those days, pleasant and agreeable and little more. He had not found himself then, but the appearance even in those days was deceptive. For he was up betimes every day and working like a beaver. Once he had the Library send over fifty volumes of railroad financing and operation. These he pored over; he learned about railroading in the hours most of his colleagues were abed.

He had been sitting at his back-row desk in the Senate Chamber four months when he introduced his first public bill. This action caused no more commotion than the falling of a leaf. It was "A Bill to provide for insurance by the Farm Credit Administration of mortgages on farm property, and for other purposes." Vice President Garner sent it to the Committee on Banking and Currency and there it died in a pigeonhole.

It was not until a lapse of more than six months that he raised his voice in Senate debate. And then it was no shout. A long bill to amend the Agricultural Adjustment Act had been under discussion for days. Guffey had offered an amendment to strike out the word barley from one provision and the Senate had turned it down. Truman addressed the Senate. What he said was brief and to the point:

"I move to reconsider the vote by which the amendment offered by the Senator from Pennsylvania . . . was rejected."

In years to come no schoolboy will be called upon to remember this maiden utterance in the Senate or to compare it with immortal words of other men who became President. But the senators within sound of Truman's voice knew what he meant. Very well, indeed, did they know; and they smacked his motion to limbo on a roll-call vote—33 Yeas, 52 Nays.

Harry Truman's grin merely widened.

During the remainder of the 1935 session, Truman took no part in debate. Not once did he lift his voice except to vote with the regulars.

"I'm not going to demagogue," he told me, "until I have something to demagogue about."

His use of the word was colloquial. Among his cronies, to demagogue meant simply to make a speech on the Senate floor. The word carried no sting, imputed nothing.

Once, and only once thereafter, in the 1935 session did Truman address the Chair. On August 15, he reported a bill on behalf of the Interstate Commerce Committee. It was a measure concerning air transport and there was a famous fight over it later. Truman had a leader's part in that fight and succeeded in amending the original bill so greatly that its daddy voted against it in its final form.

Early in his Senate career, Truman started an undertaking that occupied his time for the better part of several years. It was the sort of work he panted for—an inquiry into the causes of financial difficulties besetting some of the chief rail carriers.

Senator Wheeler of Montana, Chairman of the Interstate Commerce Committee, was author of the resolution directing the inquiry. After the Senate adopted it, Wheeler named a subcommittee of six to do the actual work, himself taking the chairmanship. Truman was the fourth, and last, Democrat on the committee.

Once more he was tail-ender Democrat on a committee,

[73]

but this time he was readied to rise and shine. At their first meeting he astonished his colleagues with his far-flung knowledge of the subject. He hadn't read those fifty books for nothing.

The delighted Wheeler made him vice chairman of the subcommittee.

It was a sort of open secret in those days that Wheeler knew all railroads were guilty of something wrong and that he suspected each was guiltier than the others. In Truman he found a disciple; and while Truman didn't go the full road of Wheeler's philosophy, he did go along for at least two looks and a jump.

Truman had been boning up on earlier testimony, much of it musty from long storage in file rooms, of swag, corruption, and remote control of the rails by banking and holding companies. It held him with a sort of fascination to learn more; and it jolted his ideas of rectitude along the pathway of his former suspicions. From the intensive perusal he emerged with a snort and a purpose.

He went into the inquiry intent on ridding the rails of sin, if possible, for long years to come. From voracious reading and, to a high degree, from personal shrewdness, he knew where to hit the trail of the sinners and how to track them down. Wheeler observed him in action and turned the investigation over to him, doubtless feeling he couldn't do a better job himself.

Under Truman's coldly calm yet always courteous investigation, rail sinning turned out to have been quite a scandalous affair.

Big fry and small from Wall Street's temples rolled down to Washington serene in the belief that some things, after all, were known only to themselves and God; rolled back to New York disillusioned, their cherished ill-doings naked to the world's cold eyes. A mild-mannered, self-effacing inquisitor from Missouri, presiding at the inquisition, had cut through to the meaty kernel of their misdeeds.

That sort of cruelty to financiers dragged along for several years. It ended finally in a rewritten rail law, the Transportation Act of 1940, governing carrier regulation and operations. It was a compromise law that Truman helped in great degree to write. From Truman's viewpoint it left uncovered some of the financial misdeeds he brought to light, but it was a long step in his direction.

Approximately eighteen months after this inquiry started, Truman made his first report to the Senate. He and Max Lowenthal wrote it. Lowenthal was an experienced cross-examiner who with evident relish helped make rail witnesses squirm. The report reeked with the philosophy of Truman during his early days in the Senate. Here are some excerpts:

"New York bankers and investment bankers seem to obstruct railroad operation. . . . Some of the greatest railroads have been deliberately looted by their financial agents. . . . Laws have been evaded . . . actually broken by railroad holding companies and New York bankers. . . . Control of 23,000 miles of railroad bandied about like a plug horse . . . Plain grafter. . . ."

And finally this:

"When one of these great transportation companies fails, lawyers and investment bankers sit around like vultures at the death of an elephant. . . . They get all the flesh, and the stockholders and public get the bones. . . ."

[75]

The Wrecking Crew, as Truman called Big Finance, knew of his hostility long before he delivered his rail report. Before he had been in the Senate three months, the big bankers knew where he stood.

They found that out in the hot fight over the Wheeler-Rayburn bill. That measure became the Public Utility Holding Company Act of 1935. It was written downtown, with Franklin Roosevelt's active blessing, by Ben Cohen, co-worker of Thomas G. Corcoran, "Tommy, the Cork," in drafting New Deal reform laws. It was sponsored in the Senate by the Chairman of Truman's Interstate Commerce Committee, and in the House by Sam Rayburn who then was Chairman of the Committee on Interstate and Foreign Commerce. It carried the death sentence to public utility holding companies.

A mammoth lobby was formed to fight it. Wendell Willkie, head of Commonwealth and Southern, participated in the fight.

The lobby's headquarters were in the fashionable Mayflower Hotel and its ramifications extended all over the United States. From a craftsman's standpoint, it was the perfect lobby. Abundantly financed, directed by the industry's best brains, it derived great political strength from its millions of security holders. It reached into the urban places and the farms alike; thus it was handsomely equipped to put pressure on Congress.

This lobby hoped to bring Harry Truman into line against the bill through the Democratic organization in Missouri. It had an ally in the *Journal-Post* in which Henry L. Doherty, head of the Cities Service group, had purchased half interest a few years before. Laurence Dickey, the publisher, and his family associates held the other half interest and directed the newspaper's policies.

When Doherty wanted anything printed in the *Journal-Post* he was required, under his contract, to sign it. Dickey was sympathetic with Doherty in opposing the public utility holding company bill, but he was in the publishing business, not public utilities, and his editorials opposing the bill were temperate.

Thus at the outset of his senatorial career Truman found himself in unhappy position with respect to the bill. His friendly home-town newspaper opposed it; party loyalty and his personal convictions impelled him to support it.

The lobby sent emissaries to the Democratic organization in Missouri to exert pressure on Truman in that quarter. It also sent emissaries direct to Truman at Washington in an attempt to convert him. Failing in both moves, it turned on pressure from his constituents at home. Missouri bombarded him with letters and telegrams.

"Look at the mess of stuff I got this morning," he said to me one day, pointing to a desk heaped with letters and telegrams. "More than two thousand since yesterday."

On the showdown Truman voted for the bill. That was all right with the *Journal-Post,* although both owners would have preferred otherwise. But it decidedly was not all right with one of the *Journal-Post's* editorial writers. He felt highly aggrieved and planted an editorial in two-column measure on the first page.

The tone of this editorial was intemperate. It flayed Truman for voting for the bill. I was in his office when the postman brought the paper in, and I read the editorial with amazement. Then Truman and I read it together.

"It's all right, Bill," he assured me. "It doesn't mean a thing to me. You see, I know it was necessary."

I was mystified.

"I don't understand what you mean by that," I said.

"Now, don't try to play innocent with me," he chided, his good-humored grin wreathing his face. "You and I both know the newspapers have to print things like that from time to time; that's the only way they can increase their circulation. If they didn't print scandals and attack people they would go out of business."

He really meant it. By further questioning, I learned that he had come to Washington with the expectation of being attacked by the press. Also that he was mildly surprised that the *Journal-Post* hadn't attacked him earlier; and that he looked forward to "a lot of attacks later on."

They wouldn't make him unhappy, he added, "because I know why they are made."

From that belief I couldn't budge him. The incident had a sequel, wholly unexpected, that put Harry Truman in a new light in my eyes and regard. The editorial writer left the paper not long after he had written that editorial. Months later I heard he was in financial straits; then for a long time I heard nothing of him.

"What became of him?" I asked Truman about a year later.

"Why, I heard he had a job in Kansas City."

"A job with the *Star?*"

"No; I believe not."

"With some other publication?"

"No; he was out of the publishing business."

That was always the teasing tack Truman would take

with me when he tried, in his overwhelming self-efface-
ment, to withhold from me something that might reflect
credit on himself. So I bored in.

"Have you heard of him recently?"

"Fairly recently."

"How recently?"

"Within a couple of weeks, I should say."

"Do you know where he's working?"

"Yes."

"Where?"

"Oh, he has a little job with the County."

That, of course, meant Jackson County whose affairs
Truman had directed before coming to the Senate.

"A little job with the County," I repeated. "Did you, by
any chance, get him that job, Harry Truman?"

"No, I can't say I did," Truman replied in evident embarrassment. "All I did was to recommend him for it."

Chapter Five

———————————✳———————————

FROM the Senate's rough-and-tumble debates over the multi-faceted New Deal program, Harry Truman stayed almost conspicuously aloof during his first senatorial term. Bills written downtown and sent by the President to Capitol Hill for enactment were roaring through the legislative mill and onto the lawbooks in rapid-fire succession. A social revolution was in the making, a revolution to Truman's keen' liking. Yet he left the polemics to his colleagues and usually was content only to have his vote recorded.

When his voice was heard it was to answer to his name on roll call. But for one outstanding exception his vote always was the Party-line vote. That exception was staged early in his career, in 1936, when Presidential opposition to advancing the payment date for the soldier bonus clashed with his sense of justice for his World War buddies. Truman voted for the bill, and when the bill was vetoed he voted to override the veto. With his aid, the veterans got their bonus money far ahead of the maturity date on their certificates.

For the six years starting with 1935 and ending with 1940, his first term in the Senate, Truman's voting record was a record of unwavering support of all New Deal bills.

It was in Truman's first year as senator that the Wagner Labor Relations Act, launching the Federal Government upon the stormy sea of management-labor discord, was passed. The Senate rang with the crusading fire of the bill's advocates and warmed from the brimstone of its opponents. To the hot debate Truman contributed no syllable, but he voted for the bill.

The Social Security Act went onto the lawbooks the same year. Its New Deal supporters heralded it as a seven-league stride toward freedom from want; its opponents damned it as an actuarially fantastic experiment pointing to a mammoth, far-flung bureaucracy. Truman was heart and soul for the experiment. He saw only its objective; his unfamiliarity with fiscal affairs denied him a crucible in which to analyze the means whereby the objective was to be attained. He spoke neither for the bill nor against it. He merely voted for it.

In less than four years after its passage, the Social Security Act confirmed counts in its opponents' indictment. More perhaps than any other enactment of the Roosevelt regime, it bore the perfume of the New Deal's extraordinary fiscal confusion. Its avowed objectives included freedom from want for the aged, but it was the only law Congress had ever passed that operated to increase the national debt by the payment of taxes into the Federal Treasury. The bigger the tax collections, the greater the national debt. Such was its formula then and so it is today. Moreover it had the luscious virtue of providing the free-spending Congress with hundreds of millions of dollars annually to allocate. This was done by the device of treating the payroll tax collections as current funds and simply placing an I.O.U. in the till (in the form of special Government bonds) to cover the moneys so spent.

Four years' operation of this law helped mightily to swell the national debt. It rose by billions and promised to rise even more rapidly as the progressively increasing tax rates became effective. A trust fund composed wholly of those I.O.U.'s and mounting to forty billion dollars lay in prospect and so did an herculean bureaucracy.

To even the dullards in Congress, it was patent that the time had come to change the formula. And changed it was by law in 1939; not altogether but to a degree that braked the rate of the rising debt. Truman voted for the change, as he voted for the original formula, without contributing to the debate. His ideas were embodied vaguely in an address to the Missouri legislature in March of that year.

"Our social security legislation may not be perfect," he said, "but it is a step in the right direction. No one wants to repeal it. It is an effort to give the everyday citizen who works for a living some hope and security that he won't be a burden in his declining years."

Further experience again demonstrated the need of changing the law. Four times in consecutive year after year Congress froze the payroll tax rate at its original figure. Even so, the trust fund in the Treasury swept past the seven billion dollar mark, all in those I.O.U.'s. The national debt is more than seven billion dollars higher than it would be otherwise. Another revision of the law is contemplated as this is written; and Harry Truman, as President, may have to accept or disapprove soon sweeping revisions in another law he helped enact.

American adherence to the World Court, sought by Roosevelt in 1935, likewise won Truman's vote. Truman took no part in the Senate debate over this measure's passage.

There were other fateful laws enacted that year. The great experiment in the Tennessee River valley was under way in 1935. Roosevelt asked Congress to strengthen the hands of the Tennessee Valley Authority and Truman again voted without question or debate—for the legislation.

In later years Truman found the Tennessee Valley setup not altogether to his liking. That was when a move was made to duplicate TVA for the Missouri River basin. Truman enlisted the technical aid of a young Army Engineer, Lewis Pick, when that move was pending and together they worked out a substitute plan for the proposed Missouri Valley Authority.

That was before America's entry into World War II. When the Pearl Harbor disaster projected the United States into the conflict, MVA legislation was laid aside and Pick was sent to the Orient where he supervised the construction of a road into China to take the place of the road closed by the Japanese. Pick's Pike was its nickname.

Early in 1945, nearly ten years after Truman had voted to strengthen TVA, the Missouri basin project was revived. Truman was Vice President then, presiding over the Senate.

Senator Murray of Montana sponsored the revived MVA bill. His measure was patterned in large part after the TVA legislation Truman had voted, as Senator, to strengthen. Truman referred the Murray bill to the Commerce Committee generally regarded as hostile to such legislation. Murray had asked that it be referred to his friendly Committee on Agriculture and Forestry. When the astonished Murray found that his bill had been routed to the camp of its opponents, he sought to have it re-referred to the Committee on Agriculture and Forestry.

He was a few minutes late in making the move. Vice President Truman had left the Senate Chamber; there was another Presiding Officer. The Truman reference stood.

After a period of delay, Murray's bill was sent on a sort of ring-around-a-rosy excursion to three committees, each of which was privileged to hold it sixty days for consideration. The triple reference was its knell. Cloakrooms echoed gossip that Truman had made the original reference with intent to kill it, anyhow.

While the Senate was speculating over the unusual situation, I chanced to meet Truman in the Senate subway. Colonel Harry Vaughan was with him. A deluge of other valley authority bills was in prospect; one, proposing a Savannah River Authority, had just been introduced.

"I see," I said to him, "that the Senate is breaking out in a rash of valley authority bills."

"Yes," said the Vice President, "we are getting bills for this river and that river and the other river. Before this thing is over I imagine we'll be getting bills to cover a lot of Republican rivers as well."

"Such as the Wabash," interjected Vaughan.

"My problem, Mr. Vice President," I said, "is this: When are you going to get around to doing something for the creeks?"

"The creeks?" Truman repeated. "Is that what you said?"

"Yes, sir; the creeks. You see, I'm up one of those creeks without a paddle, and I just wondered how long I'd have to wait until you could get around to my case."

Truman laughed heartily. He was kind enough to devote a few minutes to telling me in some detail of the plans he and Colonel Pick had developed for the Missouri Valley Authority.

"Dams where there ought to be dams. Navigation where there ought to be navigation and nowhere else; we don't want to burden the Government forever with dredging expenses. Power plants where there ought to be power plants. And all of them administered efficiently."

Such was the gist, as I gathered it, of the Truman-Pick plan for improvement of the Missouri River Basin.

The Public Utility Holding Company Act, previously mentioned in these pages, was another New Deal law passed in 1935. Truman voted for it, but took no part in the bitter debate on the floor of the Senate. The Guffey-Snyder Coal Act likewise won his vote that year, without comment. Still another bill, in which he believed completely, was a measure to extend Federal help to tenant farmers desiring to buy the fields they tilled. Truman voted for it but took no part in the debate preceding passage.

Opponents of the New Deal program united that year in two major attempts to stem the legislative tide. In one move they sought to lop two billion dollars from the pump-priming, relief appropriation of nearly five billions. In the other, they attempted to have the anti-trust laws restored to their full effectiveness; they had been set aside temporarily to remove obstacles from the program of the National Recovery Administration.

Truman voted against both. He took no part in debate.

In 1936, his second year in the Senate, Truman was as silent as before. Again he voted the Party line on legislation coming before him.

One of the bills before the Senate in 1936 concerned the plight of the nation's farmers. The Supreme Court had decided the original Triple A (Agricultural Adjustment Administration) law was unconstitutional and thereby had terminated the payment of hundreds of millions of dollars annually in farm subsidies.

On the ruins of the Court's decision, the New Deal Administration projected the Soil Conservation Act. Under its terms, the subsidies were to continue but the formula was different. Like the old law, the new one restricted production through the device of paying subsidies to farmers complying with the Washington program.

Truman again cast an impulsive vote. It was for the new proposal. What he may have thought about it was not divulged in Senate debate. In a radio address delivered in March, 1936, he said:

"The Administration is making an honest effort to create a definite policy for agriculture, one which will place the farmer on a level with other industries.

"For the first time in our history, we are discovering that the producer of food and fiber is a vital and essential part of our population, and that his interests and welfare are as important as the banker's, the manufacturer's and the building contractor's.

"The welfare of the country demands that this policy should be carried to a successful conclusion and I am sure that the country as a whole will see that it is."

He was not so sure about that three years later, however. During those three intervening years, the subsidies of many millions annually failed to bring prosperity down on the farm. Once more a New Deal revision bill was up in the Senate. Under his Party-line voting policy, Truman supported it.

The doubts that had crept into his mind were spread before the Senate then. In an address on March 2, 1939, Truman said:

"The farm problem in the Middle West and the South is becoming more difficult. I am very much interested and anxious to find a solution.

"There is no desire on my part to be critical or to question the motives of Secretary [of Agriculture] Wallace and his various farm remedies. The farm bill as passed by the last Congress apparently is not working successfully.

"Whether that is due to the legislation itself or its administration, I do not know. But the fact remains that income to the farmer has not been materially increased. The farmer is not getting his fair share of the national income, and unless he can get his fair share there is no settlement of the problem."

The new proposal Harry Truman voted for in 1939 was to plaster another farm mortgage on public funds in the Treasury. This was in the form of an additional grant up to $225,000,000 a year in so-called parity payments to farmers producing any of four crops: wheat, corn, rice, and tobacco.

Three weeks after voicing his doubts to the Senate, Truman repeated them to the Missouri legislature.

"The Roosevelt Administration," he said, "has made an honest effort to help the farmer, but I am not convinced that the present AAA is working in the interest of the man for whom it was created. There have been too much red tape and paper work and too much recognition of the men who farm the farmer. . . .

"Our ideas of land uses must be revamped. Marginal and submarginal land now cultivated must be put to other uses—reforestation, wild-life preserves, and in some cases just plain abandonment and let Nature take her course.

"Soil conservation . . . ought to be continually carried forward. All the money spent on the whole farm program isn't a drop in the bucket when compared to the soil depletion of the last fifty years. There isn't a reason in the world why soil conservation and the domestic allotment plan, or some other practical plan, would not work together."

Not long thereafter, World War II changed the farmer's plight. Drab poverty gave way to record income. But the New Deal program prior to the war failed utterly to produce a formula that solved the farmer's troubles. For a decade, as Senator Truman, he faithfully followed that program despite his doubts.

Now the war is over. The farm problem, in somewhat different guise, is on its way to Truman again. Soon he probably will have to approve or reject a formula worked out by Republicans. But the problem itself is neither Republican nor Democratic; it is as non-political as Death or Taxes. When the problem reaches him for the fourth time, he cannot dismiss it by simply following the Party line as he did three times before.

In 1936, his second year in the Senate, Truman became interested in two remarkable New Deal proposals. The first was a project involving the construction of a ship canal across the Florida peninsula. The second was a vision of harnessing the tides at Passamaquoddy. Neither matured, although public funds were spent for work on both. Truman voted to authorize studies on each.

Congress adjourned that year on the eve of the opening of the Democratic National Convention at Philadelphia. On the last night of the session Truman had a new and not altogether happy experience.

As usual, a considerable number of bills had been left for Senate action the last day of the session. These were being passed under a unanimous-consent arrangement. A bill would be called up and its passage moved. The Presiding Officer would say:

"Is there objection? The Chair hears none and the bill is passed."

Objection by a single senator would prevent a bill's passage.

Among the bills unacted upon was one which had been sponsored in the House by Representative Healey and in the Senate by Senator Walsh, both of Massachusetts. Earlier in the year, the House had passed it. The Senate had not acted on it. Under its terms the Secretary of Labor (Miss Perkins) would have been authorized to require

Government contractors to pay the "prevailing wage" on projects involving $10,000 or more. The Secretary would have determined the "prevailing wage."

Considerable opposition to this bill had developed in both business and labor groups. Missouri's senators, Clark and Truman, were among its opponents. They suspected that an attempt would be made on the last day of the session to have the Senate pass the bill under unanimous consent. So they decided to remain on the floor until adjournment in order to object if the bill were called up.

The session dragged on past the dinner hour. Shortly after eight o'clock, when only a few senators were in the Chamber, Truman told Clark he was going to slip downstairs to the restaurant for a quick dinner.

"I wasn't gone more than twenty minutes," Truman told me the next day on our drive to Philadelphia from Washington. "When I came back I saw that Clark wasn't in the Chamber. I then found that Walsh had called the bill up and that it had passed, without objection, only a minute or so before I got back. It was too late then, of course, to do anything about it."

"Where was Clark?" I asked.

"It had slipped his mind completely and he had stepped into the cloakroom for a few minutes. It was while he was out of the Chamber that the bill was called up and passed. To make it worse, some of our friends were sitting in the gallery and saw the whole thing. I can imagine how they felt."

Although Truman had little to say in Senate debate during his first two years as Senator, he was exceedingly busy with his work in committees. It was in that period that he started his investigation of the railroads and laid the foundation for the new Transportation Act. The investigation went far to confirm his belief that what he loosely called Wall Street preyed upon the little people of the nation.

He expounded this philosophy from the Senate floor several times thereafter. In a remarkable address to the Senate in December, 1937, he said:

"One of the difficulties as I see it is that we worship money instead of honor. A billionaire in our estimation is much greater in the eyes of the people than the public servant who works for the public interest.

"It makes no difference if the billionaire rode to wealth on the sweat of little children and the blood of underpaid labor.

"No one ever considers Carnegie libraries steeped in the blood of the Homestead steel workers, but they are. We do not remember that the Rockefeller Foundation is founded on the dead miners of the Colorado Fuel & Iron Company and a dozen other similar performances. We worship Mammon. Until we go back to the ancient fundamentals and return to the Giver of the Tables of the Law and His teachings, these conditions are going to remain with us.

"It is a pity that Wall Street with its ability to control all the wealth of the nation and to hire the best brains of the country has not produced some statesmen, some men who could see the dangers of bigness and of the concentration of the control of wealth. Instead of working to meet the situation, they are still employing the best law brains to serve greed and selfish interest.

"People can stand only so much, and one of these days

there will be a settlement. We shall have one receivership too many, one unnecessary depression out of which we will not come with the power still in the same old hands.

"I believe the country would be better off if we did not have sixty percent of the assets of all insurance companies concentrated in four companies. I believe that a thousand insurance companies with $4,000,000 each in assets would be just a thousand times better for the country than the Metropolitan Life with $4,000,000,000 in assets. The average human brain is not built to deal with such astronomical figures.

"I say also that a thousand county-seat towns of 7,000 people each are a thousand times more important to this Republic than one city of 7,000,000. Our unemployment and our unrest are the result of the concentration of wealth, the concentration of population in industrial centers, mass production, and a lot of other so-called modern improvements.

"We are building a Tower of Babel."

This address won wide applause in organized labor circles. Those were the halcyon days of his senatorship when Harry Truman was called by some, "the best friend Labor ever had in the Senate." So, at least, he was appraised then by one big segment of Labor, the railroad unions. Other segments admired him, too, and regarded him as an ally. But Labor's appraisal of Truman, like many an appraisal of other pressure groups, was not wholly accurate either then or after he became President.

In his first Senate term he championed the cause of Labor again and again, but he was not blind to its mistakes. Among these, he thought, was the sit-down strike.

When it first was adopted, in Detroit in 1937, Truman cast his vote for a measure sponsored by Senator Byrnes condemning it. The sit-down strike, Truman thought, was beyond the pale of a fair industrial fight; he attributed it to the machinations of leaders who would stop at nothing to win their row.

But he was strong for Labor's rank and file. These he considered generally overworked and underpaid. So when the Fair Labor Standards Act came before the Senate in 1937 Truman supported it warmly, though he refrained from taking part in the debate. Roosevelt's poetic description of that Act, "A floor under wages and a ceiling on hours," captivated him. The floor was low and the ceiling high, in his opinion, for the first few years of the Act's operation; but as the one was lowered and the other rose, the standards approached gradually his ideas of partial justice.

They never fully satisfied him. Again and again while Senator, Truman moved toward higher compensation for the men and women who labored. As President, he repeatedly urged Congress to increase the minimum-wage rate. He also advocated legislation to increase unemployment compensation pay.

One of the New Deal measures warmly supported by Labor in 1937 was the Bituminous Coal Act which had been sponsored by Senator Guffey of Pennsylvania. Under this law, the Government moved in to supervise closely the financial affairs of the soft-coal industry. The mine owners remained in possession of their properties and operated them under the Government's formula. Under this elaborate plan, the Government fixed not only minimum prices

[93]

of each kind of bituminous coal on the market, but fixed as well the minimum prices each mine could charge.

Mine owners were divided in sentiment as to the wisdom of this law, but the miners were solidly behind it. And no wonder! For it provided that no bituminous coal should be sold below cost of production and that cost was heavily loaded with labor. Enactment operated to prevent any decrease in wages; and it certainly put no obstacle in the way of annual wage increases. John L. Lewis and his United Mine Workers, then in good grace at the White House, held the Act in high favor.

Truman took no part in the debate, but cast his vote for the measure. It remained on the statute books approximately six years and expired by limitation. Never close to Lewis at any time, Truman simply followed the Party line in supporting the legislation.

Roosevelt's plan to place the Civilian Conservation Corps on a permanent basis, placed before Congress in 1937, fell in the same general category. It sought to extend the Government's aid to the hundreds of thousands of young men enlisted in 1933 and thereafter. With that objective Truman was in hearty accord. His vote was cast for the measure.

Another bill for which Truman impulsively cast his vote in 1937 was the ill-starred Neutrality Act. This came back twice to Congress thereafter for revision. When it was enacted, the bloody Civil War in Spain was at its height. Subsequent events strongly indicated that enactment of this law doomed the Spanish Republic and contributed greatly to the establishment of the Franco regime.

There was strong pressure, backed by forces of great

political power, which never appeared on the surface of events for the passage of the Neutrality Act. There also was much sentiment against it. The opponents, however, were not so closely knit or so well organized as the advocates. Truman's colleague, Bennett Clark, took a leading role in piloting this legislation through the Senate. Clark was one of the small group that organized the American Legion soon after the end of World War I. With the grim tragedies of that epochal struggle in mind, he was active in seeking to prevent his country from being drawn into further clashes in Europe.

The Neutrality Act was designed to keep America clear of the fighting in Spain. It did so, at a price. Part of the price was to tie America's hands when the thunderhead of World War II darkened European skies. When the war broke in 1939, the Act's revision became imperative. Truman voted then for revision.

He was to hear still more of the Neutrality Act, however. In 1941, when it had become abundantly clear that Britain was fighting for her very existence and that only American aid could save her, a further revision amounting to the Act's repeal was proposed. That, too, won Truman's vote.

Virtually all legislation before Congress in 1937 related to America's internal affairs; true to form, Truman cast his vote for New Deal measures without question. One of the measures coming before Congress that year, however, concerned America's foreign affairs as well.

This was the Trade Agreements Act which delegated to the President the power to make trade agreements with foreign countries. These had the force of treaties. Under them, protective tariff duties prescribed by Congress in

1930 could be lowered; the theory being that nations thus afforded more advantageous entry to American markets would reciprocate by making easier the entry of American products into their markets.

The President was given the power to lower the rates without further reference to Congress.

The original grant was enacted in 1934 and was limited to a life of three years. Under it, Roosevelt made such agreements, lowering many duties. The policy was announced as a policy to increase America's foreign trade, but the agreements themselves were objected to violently by certain groups of American producers. Large numbers of manufacturers supported the policy; large segments of farmers opposed it.

Like nearly all other major New Deal laws, the Trade Agreements Act broke with American traditions. For the first time in its history, Congress surrendered the right to fix the rates of tariffs and delegated such power to the President. Cordell Hull, Secretary of State, fathered the policy and administered it with Roosevelt's acclaim.

Before the Act was to expire by limitation, in 1937, a three-year extension was sought by the President. Congress readily voted the extension; Truman cast his vote for it. Three years later, in 1940, when the life of the extended law neared its end, a further extension was requested. It, too, was voted. At that time Truman not only supported continuance but addressed the Senate, for the first time on the subject, and taunted the Act's opponents.

"It seems self-evident," he told the Senate in March, 1940, "that if the trade-agreements program has in fact been injurious to American agriculture, as claimed, opponents of the proposal to extend its operation another three years would produce facts and figures to support their charges.

"None has been produced. Why? The answer is simple, because in reality domestic agriculture has been aided by the trade-agreements program."

Senator Truman then made this highly significant statement respecting his tariff views:

"The tariff is a highly complicated and technical question which unhappily has been used in the past to serve political ends at cross purposes with national welfare.

"The present Administration in 1934 took the lead in world commercial relations in an intelligent and practical manner and placed the adjustment of tariff duties in the hands of the most competent men available for the purpose, men beyond the reach of political logrolling and tariff lobbying at the expense of national welfare."

The three-year extension was voted again in 1940. When it was about to expire once more (in 1943) Congress, with Truman supporting the move, extended the law for a third time. On that occasion, the extension was for two years, ending in June, 1945.

In 1945, Truman as President sought another extension. His party was supreme in both Houses and voted continuance. The law was extended until June, 1948. Moreover, to afford the President greater bargaining facilities in fashioning trade agreements with other countries for the postwar period, Congress gave him additional power. It authorized him to cut tariff rates, at his discretion, but not to exceed fifty percent below their levels of January, 1945.

The rates effective in January, 1945, in many cases were

far below those prescribed by Congress in 1930, thanks to successive trade agreements since 1934. Opponents of the policy made much quarrelsome ado over the prospect of further reductions. The issue grew in importance as the time for holding the International Trade Conference in 1947 approached.

Republicans then had assumed control of Congress. They were divided in sentiment over the trade-agreements policy. Many Democrats also had veered away from it. The issue cut across Party lines.

Once more, after many years, the protective tariff loomed as a leading issue in a Presidential election campaign. And once more, Harry Truman as President, heard the echo of a Senate speech.

The year 1937 produced deep, but temporary, cleavage in the Democratic party over Roosevelt's Supreme Court packing plan. Bennett Clark, senior senator from Missouri, was a leader in the fight against the plan. Harry Truman, junior senator from Missouri, supported Roosevelt.

In that year, Roosevelt nominated Hugo Black, a senator from Alabama, to be an Associate Justice of the Supreme Court. Black's enemies charged that he had been a member years before of the Ku Klux Klan in Alabama and opposed his confirmation largely on that ground.

The New Deal Senate confirmed the nomination. Truman again followed the Party line and voted for confirmation.

Chapter Six

———————✳———————

IN JANUARY, 1938, when the Seventy-fifth Congress met for its second session, Harry Truman was ready to let the Senate hear his Missouri drawl in debate.

He had learned the ropes. For three years at his last-row desk he had listened until his eardrums ached. Now he would exercise his own vocal cords. He would have something to say from time to time; plenty, especially, about Wall Street and its devils.

But he had nothing to say about the big issue on every tongue in the Capitol except his, the issue that raged like a brush fire in autumn. Second only to the uproar over the court-packing proposal of the year before, the new controversy centered on another Roosevelt idea, the so-called reorganization program. The new fight was widening and deepening the party rift of 1937; almost half of the Democrats were in open rebellion and Roosevelt's leadership, sunk to its lowest level, was drifting still lower.

Truman had no desire to mix in that mess. His inquiry

into railroad troubles and other subjects engrossed him. Even had he wanted to enter the debate, he hardly had time to analyze the issue before leveling his verbal lance. But this much he did know: Roosevelt had asked for reorganization and good old Jim Farley was working to put it across. That was enough. Jim could count on him.

What Roosevelt wanted had been put on paper by Louis Brownlow, a protégé of Woodrow Wilson. Brownlow had served a term as Commissioner of the District of Columbia and subsequently had withdrawn from public office to make an intensive study of Government's financial affairs.

The Brownlow report was an amazing document. It proposed that Congress delegate to the President power to reshuffle the entire executive establishment, shifting agencies wherever he wanted, abolishing some of them if he wished, and creating a new Department of Welfare whose Secretary would sit in the Cabinet.

Moreover, it called for loosening the congressional grip on the national purse strings and giving the President latitude to spend widely, subject only to post-audit by an Auditor-General. In effect, Congress was to go away back and sit down. Reasons for the proposed new arrangement were two: Economy and efficiency.

Many a Democrat said, "Nuts to that."

And many another in serious vein denounced the maneuver as a long step toward an American dictatorship.

O'Connor of New York, head of the powerful Rules Committee in the House, arraigned it scornfully and in biting terms. Roosevelt saw to it that O'Connor was "purged" from public life for his temerity at the next election. Along with Rayburn of Texas, then the Majority Leader, Cochran of Truman's home state carried the President's flag in the House. "Jimmy" Byrnes, who was to become Secretary of State in Truman's Cabinet, led the Roosevelt forces in the Senate.

Bennett Clark of Missouri, Truman's colleague, fought the new Roosevelt project as vigorously as he had fought the court-packing plan a year before. Jasper Bell of Missouri, congressman from the district where Truman voted back home, opposed it in the House.

The Senate was first to vote. On March 28, the Byrnes bill embodying the reorganization program reached final roll call after days of bitter debate. Before the vote was taken, a motion was made to send the bill back to committee for further study. On this test vote, opponents lost, 43 to 48. On the vote for passage of the bill the tally was 49 to 42.

Truman contributed to the seven votes that marked the narrow margin of Roosevelt's victory in the Senate. But what Truman thought of the bill he kept to himself. His only expression of opinion was in two words. The first was "Nay" on the motion to recommit; the second was "Yea" on the bill's passage.

Eleven days later the House was ready to vote. The tide of Democratic resentment there had swept to a new high mark. The feeble Republican minority of 88 members opposed the program solidly. The New Deal majority was split as badly as it had been over the court-packing proposal.

As in the Senate, a motion was made to recommit the bill.

In an atmosphere tense with suppressed emotion, the

move prevailed. The vote was 204 to 196. One hundred and sixteen Democrats united with the solid Republican minority in an anti-Roosevelt coalition, and the reorganization bill was dead by an eyelash. Truman's congressman supplied one of the eight votes that spelled the coalition's scant majority.

Thus Roosevelt's second attempt in fourteen months to fix his supremacy over the judiciary and the Congress went the way of the first. Truman had no word to say in the debate on either measure. He supported the President each time.

What Truman did have to say in the session of 1938 related chiefly to topics less torrid. And then his comments usually were brief. Sometimes they consisted of a few words only, sandwiched between remarks of the leaders. His first observation on the Senate floor that year followed this pattern. It was chaser to a question he had leveled at Reynolds of North Carolina who yielded for a question in his long address. Truman expressed the opinion that domestic troubles then prevalent in China could be attributed to a single outstanding reason. And that reason, he opined, was China's isolationism, her living for centuries to and for herself alone. "A course," he continued, "you are now advocating that the United States should follow, is it not?"

Reynolds demurred, and Truman had no more to say.

Later he spoke of the need for safety on the highways, and sponsored a bill to promote it. The bill died in committee.

He toyed with the idea that the Government should promote construction of a network of superhighways. When the Senate disapproved, he moved to reconsider the vote but left the motion dangling and did not press it. Later he had something to say on such assorted topics as the long-and-short haul practice of the railroads, automobile liens, operation of motor vehicles, and emergency relief.

Another situation that impressed him was the lack of a travel fund for congressional secretaries. Members of House and Senate received liberal mileage allowance. When an appropriation bill was in debate, Truman tried to amend it to make $65,000 available for secretarial and clerk travel. Senator Adams of Colorado was shepherding the bill to passage. He praised Truman's objective but made a point of order that the amendment would constitute new legislation attached to an appropriation bill in violation of Senate rules. The point was sustained.

As Chairman of an Interstate Commerce subcommittee, Truman addressed the Senate at length on his proposal to have the Interstate Commerce Commission regulate charges for air traffic.

"The Commission," he said, "is the rate-making body created by Congress for that purpose. If Congress does not want the Commission to make the rates, it ought to repeal the law. If, however, the Commission is going to make the rates for mail on the railroads, and other rates for carriers such as buses and trucks in every other line of transportation endeavor, the same condition ought to prevail so far as the air carriers are concerned."

Truman lost. Air regulation was turned over to the Civil Aeronautics Authority. But he was hopeful that C.A.A.'s regulation would be brief.

"I think the time will come," he said in March, 1939,

"when every method of transportation will be under the same regulatory body, and I hope it will be soon."

With remarkable clarity he foresaw the role aviation would play in war. On July 2, 1937, more than two years before the start in Europe of the conflict that became the Second World War, his address on this subject was prophetic.

"From its very inception," he said, "air transportation has been a waif in the field of commerce. It has been batted about from pillar to post and it is high time for it to be recognized as a public necessity and given a permanent place in the national transportation system.

"England, France, Germany, Russia, all realize what air transport means to national defense. Only poor old Uncle Sam is muddling with civilian air transport. This bill will stop the muddling and inaugurate a real policy—a policy which will make commercial aviation a second line of defense. . . .

"Aviation has become the eyes of the Army and the Navy, as well as a defense against bombing attacks of a possible enemy. Large numbers of trained pilots will be most essential should an emergency come. Commercial aviation will be the place to get them.

"Large production problems will face both Army and Navy in the event of war. Commercial production factories are the only sources from which we can get airplanes. We must therefore recognize the necessity of protecting and encouraging commercial aviation."

The bill was not passed in the form Truman proposed.

Yet far more than planes, Truman knew, was needed to equip the nation adequately for war. He was not one to beat the drums, but repeatedly he urged that the military and naval services be strengthened. The gist of his promptings was summarized in an address to an American Legion Post in Washington in March, 1938.

"I believe in an adequate national defense program," he said. "I think that the old Puritan who prayed regularly for protection against the Indians was much safer when, at the same time, he prudently kept his powder dry."

At long last, Truman was finding voice. More: he was polishing his homely phrases and fitting them into striking sentences that carried a metaphorical punch. For simile, he had aptness and a flair. He used it often to plaster an accent over a point.

As farm boy, clerk, and merchant Truman had learned the hard way to extract one hundred cents' performance from a dollar. The hard way seemed branded on his subconsciousness, and the branding seemed to get bigger as his senatorial service lengthened.

From time to time in his second senatorial term he spoke in the Senate to castigate the government's free spenders. Even the Army he loved was not immune: "They do a good job on the waste side," he once told the Senate; "they throw money around by the scoop shovelful."

With the ways of taxation he was far less acquainted. He had a notion, however, that a man's tax return to the Government should be held confidential, like his relations with his doctor or lawyer. This streak of individualism in his New Deal philosophy impelled him to vote the first year he came to the Senate to repeal a law giving publicity to individual income tax payments. The repealer had been introduced by his own congressman, Jasper Bell.

Two years thereafter, in 1937, Truman opposed a move to increase individual income taxes on $6,000 of income or more. Still later, when war hysteria was demanding that corporations be taxed more heavily, he voted against increasing their normal-surtax rate from forty per cent to fifty.

He opposed an overtax, whether applied to individual or corporate income. When the Senate during the war voted on a move to limit—too greatly, he thought—the profit a contractor might make on Government work, Truman helped defeat that, too. A better way to prevent too big a profit, he thought, would be by renegotiation which he supported.

His desire to have the Government give taxpayers a square deal as he saw it probably would have been more successful had he been more familiar with the subject. This was demonstrated in his move to amend the Revenue Act of 1943.

Business firms, he said, should be allowed to set aside from the heavy wartime levies special funds or reserves to be untouched during the war but designed for use in promoting peacetime production after the war's end. He introduced, a bit impulsively, an amendment he thought would turn the trick.

But he failed to think the proposal through to its end. His amendment called for tax-exemption of one-fifth of the earnings of a firm engaged in war production. The exempted fund was to be termed deferred maintenance. It should be used, he thought, for such purposes as plant expansion and replacement of wartime machinery with equipment to manufacture products for civilians. The amendment carried a formula under which the Government would supervise and regulate the spending.

A question was asked during debate on the amendment as to whether one-fifth of a firm's earnings or one-fifth of its tax should be set aside. Truman said first one and then the other. As the question was pressed, he appeared confused and failed to make the distinction clear. His fumbling helped to defeat his proposal.

The Finance Committee has preliminary supervision of all tax legislation debated in the Senate. Members of the Committee have become specialists in the intricacies of such legislation; most of the other members, like Truman at that time, do not fully understand fine tax distinctions. Because of their superior knowledge, committeemen have decided advantage in debate on taxation over other members.

Under these circumstances virtually all tax legislation passed by the Senate is mainly in the form presented by the committee. Other members have small chance of having their amendments, offered on the floor, embodied in the law. And regardless of politics, committeemen often unite to defeat such amendments.

So it was in the case of Truman's amendment. Taft of Ohio, a committeeman, contended—and virtually proved —that Truman's amendment would result in a several-billion dollar decrease in tax collections from the levels of existing law. As the bill was designed to increase taxes, he added, the Truman amendment clearly was contrary to the objective. It might better be attached to a bill to reduce taxes, rather than to increase them.

The amendment was rejected overwhelmingly.

"I still think it's a good idea," Truman told me in his office a day or so later. "It's sound and it's workable. Maybe I did ask for too much to be set aside, but that could have been changed very easily.

"My trouble was, I suppose, that I'm ignorant as a fool about taxes."

"Why not change it a bit and try it when the next tax bill comes up?" I suggested. "Maybe you didn't go about it right."

"What have I done wrong now?" he wanted to know.

"Nothing at all," I replied. "You did everything right— and you got a good licking, didn't you?"

"Did I overlook something?"

"You probably hadn't noticed it in the past," I replied, "but did it ever occur to you that nobody gets anywhere when he bucks a Finance Committee tax bill on the floor?"

"I can't say I had," he said. "I suppose you think I should have taken it up with the committee before the bill was reported."

"Exactly."

"Which committee—House or Senate?"

"Either," I suggested. "If you want to wait until the bill gets over here, take it up with the Finance Committee. If you want to get in on the ground floor, take it up with the Ways and Means Committee on the House side.

"You might even write the Chairman and tell him you want to be heard on this matter when the next tax bill comes before his committee."

"I think that's a good idea," he said, ringing for his stenographer. "Let's do it now."

He wrote Congressman Doughton, Chairman of the

Ways and Means Committee, making the request. So far as I know, Truman's letter is still in the committee's files. It was not acted on; there was no further bill to increase taxes while he was Senator.

Sometimes Truman's philosophy and ideas as to financial affairs placed him in opposition to the Roosevelt program.

America had grown great, Truman was convinced, because it had always been a Land of Opportunity where brains or brawn had fair chance to fashion their estate. He wanted no truck with a ceiling on such Opportunity. There were ceilings on prices, wages and other things and Truman had helped put them up.

Roosevelt finally placed a ceiling on Opportunity. By Executive Order issued under his vast war powers, he put a limit of $25,000 a year, after paying taxes, on the amount any person could keep for himself out of income.

There was a vast amount of grumbling about it and after a period of many months Congress debated a motion to rescind it. Truman supported this motion, which was successful. He was not so much concerned as to the amount involved as he was with the principle; he simply wanted no ceiling placed on Opportunity even in war.

Despite his failure to amend the Revenue Act of 1943, Truman voted for it. The measure was unacceptable, however, to Roosevelt who wanted more revenue, and he vetoed it. It went back to Congress with a biting message from the President that enraged some of his closest friends there. Among these was the Majority Leader of the Senate, Senator Barkley of Kentucky. Barkley made a dramatic speech to the Senate in which he resigned the Leadership.

But Roosevelt smoothed his ruffled feathers and Barkley went back to his old stand.

The House was hot, too, and overrode the veto. When it came before the Senate for action, Truman voted to override. Both Houses thus rejected Roosevelt's angry veto and the bill became law without his signature.

Tax technicalities and Truman were strangers, but the effects of heavy taxation were something else. These came home to him intimately and painfully early in World War II. Federal income taxes alone at that time amounted to one-fourth of his salary. It was toll the Truman budget was ill prepared to pay. And it came at a time when public and private demands on his purse were near their highest and rising higher.

In his quandary, Truman turned to his wife. It was an altogether instinctive turn for him to make. For just as he had helped her in her household chores, she had helped him in his public work. He seldom made an important speech without consulting her; sometimes he submitted his advance copy to her and they discussed it. And often she was at his office, an unpaid clerk, helping him when work was heavy.

The obvious need was to increase the family income. It was accomplished, to the liking of neither, by her transformation from a clerk without pay to one on the pay roll. Thereafter, she was a daily worker on Capitol Hill, at the same time continuing to supervise her household affairs—a double burden.

Truman's scorn for Wall Street bankers failed to abate in the closing years of his first term as Senator. And now that he was talking more often from the floor, he referred to their sins with fair frequency.

"Railroads are absolutely essential to the welfare of the country," was the wind-up for one of his observations (December 20, 1937) to the Senate. "We must have them for they are our most economical means of transportation today.

"I am not in favor of the Government taking them over. Wall Street seems to have failed in its management. Wall Street says the condition is the result of the depression, of paying rail labor too much, of Government regulation.

"If Government regulation and the depression brought about the present condition of the railroads, then Wall Street brought about both Government regulation and the depression. If Wall Street had produced the necessary statesmen to run the railroads, they would never have needed regulation.

"If Wall Street had dealt properly with the Interstate Commerce Commission, and the Commission had cut out private conferences with Wall Street lawyers and bankers, and not let them argue their cases in private, we might have had some sort of effective regulation of the railroads.

"Wild greed along the lines I have been describing brought on the depression. When investment bankers, so called, continually load great transportation companies with debt in order to sell securities to savings banks and insurance companies so they can make a commission, the well finally runs dry."

In the second session of the Seventy-fifth Congress he was at it again.

"There are great rail systems in this country," he told the

Senate in June, 1938, "now being operated by lawyers and engineers and accountants who could not sell gold dollars for ninety-five cents. Rail management can only see straight down the right of way as it was laid out in 1890, and all the help is in the same frame of mind. . . . What the rails need is some young blood with imagination. . . .

"Yet all the old-line railroaders see is, 'Raise rates and cut pay.' They had better follow Henry Ford and cut rates and raise pay.

"The rail-rate structure was created to fool the public and not to sell transportation. . . ."

This was nearing its end, however. In the Seventy-sixth Congress, which convened in January, 1939, Truman's subcommittee ended its long investigation. Truman, Wheeler, Max Lowenthal, and others wrote a bill changing in many respects the law governing rail regulation. The bill included provisions to regulate motor carriers and waterways, as well.

The bill was placed before the Senate in 1939. There was no great opposition to it, but there was delay in acting on it, and there was further delay in House passage. House and Senate bills differed in various respects, and there ensued a period of months during which conferees were deadlocked over these differences. A compromise was agreed upon finally, and in September, 1940, the bill was approved by the President and became law.

Throughout the long deadlock, Truman stuck with his measure, yielding slowly and grudgingly when the House conferees were adamant, adamant himself when he felt an important principle was involved. Had it not been for his patience and skill it is doubtful if the Transportation Act of 1940 would have reached the lawbook.

Truman lambasted rail management of fiscal affairs during the long period of the law's gestation, but he was aware of the carriers' desperate needs from time to time. And he was not so cool to those needs as to deny a modicum of relief.

The carriers, he was sure, had got themselves into an unholy mess because of Wall Street's domination. But when he was presented an opportunity to throw them a lifeline, he threw it. It was on his motion that the Senate amended the law to let Reconstruction Finance Corporation succor them by purchasing rail obligations.

What the Wall Street bankers he hated could not do or would not, Truman had the Government do. Several hundred million dollars of RFC loans saved the day for more than one big railroad system teetering on the brink of bankruptcy; and such loans helped ease the tough trip of others down the Hard Times right of way. Most of these loans subsequently were repaid and the Government made a tidy profit on them. It borrowed the money from the public at about two per cent a year interest and loaned the same money to the railroads at four per cent.

All of which went to show that Harry Truman knew a thing or two about finance even if he were "ignorant as a fool" about taxes. Over the long period of its operation, Reconstruction Finance Corporation made a profit approximating half a billion dollars on loans. Some of that profit can be attributed to railroad loans.

Throughout 1939 Truman continued to follow faithfully

the Party line in all legislation coming before the Senate.

That was the year that Roosevelt nominated his pal, Harry Hopkins, to be Secretary of Commerce. Many a Democrat held this Prince of Spenders utterly unfitted for the post, and the conservative business concerns the Department supposedly served generally were inclined to gag at the thought of Secretary Hopkins.

Truman voted for Hopkins' confirmation.

When the President's remaining power to devalue the gold content of the dollar was about to expire by limitation, Truman joined the Senate's New Deal majority in voting an extension. And when an additional grant of more than a billion and a half dollars for public works was sought by Roosevelt, Truman voted for that, too.

Once again (in 1939) Truman voted to authorize construction of the Florida ship canal. He also supported a bill to expand the current low-cost housing program. Both proposals came to Congress with Roosevelt's blessing.

Truman now was of the Senate's inner New Deal circle, a tested group upon whose votes Jim Farley and the President could rely. His loyalty to the President was stronger and healthier now than it had been in the unhappy, wavering days of 1937 when he complained that Roosevelt was treating him "like an office boy." His loyalty to his friends in the Senate was no less devoted. He knew now the heady fellowship of that senatorial courtesy he had scorned to invoke a year earlier when he denounced Maurice Milligan on the Senate floor.

He had not asked that for himself when Milligan's name came up, but he was willing freely to extend it, even in opposition to Roosevelt. And such an opportunity presented

[114]

itself in 1939 when Floyd H. Roberts was nominated to be a Federal judge in Virginia.

Mr. Roberts' nomination was opposed by Carter Glass and Harry Byrd, Virginia's senators. Truman was not particularly close to either of them. Glass was too old to fit in with the fun-making of Truman's widening circle of buddies, and Byrd was of a wholly different temperament. Yet when the Old Dominion's senators invoked senatorial courtesy to junk the Roberts nomination, Truman was right there to extend it without delay or question. He was keen to oblige Farley and Roosevelt, but he was keener to observe the Senate's good fellowship rule. With the help of Truman's vote, Roberts was rejected.

Another proposal Truman didn't care for emanated from the so-called silver bloc in the Senate.

This small bi-partisan group from the West and Far West was compact and powerful. It worshiped politically not at the shrine of the golden calf but the silver pig. Its purpose was to feed the pig aplenty by maintaining silver at high prices through direct Government subsidy in the form of a Treasury bonus, above the world market price, for every fine ounce mined. The feeding was done with disgust by Treasury officials; indeed, Henry Morgenthau, the Department's head, was in hot water much of his long term because of his feud with the silver bloc.

The pig opened its mouth again in 1939 for another juicy bite at the general taxpayers' expense. The proposal was to raise the Treasury price to 77.57 cents an ounce for all newly mined domestic silver. Truman voted to shut the pig's mouth.

By that time probably every senator this side of the

Pearly Gates knew Harry Truman was no friend of the private electric power magnates. He had shown that again and again; and no less often he had shown, as well, that he had a strong sense of what was just and right. The two manifestations came to a magnificent clash in 1939 and the sense of justice prevailed. The issue was a proposal to let Tennessee Valley Authority issue $100,000,000 in bonds so that it might buy up private power facilities. Truman couldn't see it. Notwithstanding his dislike for the magnates, he voted "Nay."

It was about this time, while he was floating along happily on the New Deal tide and taking a day off now and then to crack a few heads in Wall Street, that Truman was given the keys to the city of Hagerstown, Maryland.

The circumstances under which this honor was extended probably had never been duplicated in the past and are unlikely to occur in the future.

It happened of a Sunday noon. Truman was driving back in his little car from Kansas City to Washington. His wife and daughter were with him. There were only a few delights he enjoyed more than motoring, and one of those was faster motoring. He would streak out of Washington early of a morning and get his dinner, likely as not, the evening of the next day in Kansas City, halfway across the continent. He drove with great skill, but his speed was not calculated to appeal to timid old ladies.

Down the narrow streets of Hagerstown came Truman, all aglow and feeling fine. The sun was shining, the air was tonic, and the town was at church. A long line of cars was parked on the street he traveled. Where it joined the main artery of traffic, there was a STOP sign.

[116]

Truman didn't see it. In a jiffy after he had turned into the main highway, the air was full of horrible noise, crumpled fenders, cracked gears, broken glass and much mechanical confusion. The Truman family stepped from the wreckage, virtually unhurt but much annoyed. So did the other fellow he had bumped.

Two policemen came up on the run. When they found nobody was hurt badly, they waved the drivers to the sidewalk and asked to see permits.

They were not impressed by the other fellow's permit. When they saw Truman's, they went into a huddle.

"It says here," one of them addressed Truman, "that you're a United States Senator. Is that right, mister?"

"That's right," Truman replied, flashing his infectious grin sheepishly.

They went back into the huddle. Presently one of them walked away and the other came back to Truman.

"You don't mind waiting a few minutes, do you, Senator?" he asked. "You see, it's the first time we ever saw a Senator pull one like this, and we thought we'd better tell the Mayor. The other officer has gone to get him; he's over yonder in that church."

Truman waited. Presently the policeman returned. The Mayor was with him.

"Senator Truman?" asked the Mayor, introducing himself.

Truman acknowledged his identity and added his regrets over having caused the Mayor and his efficient policemen so much trouble. The trouble was, he explained, that a parked car had obscured the STOP sign and he had gone past it without seeing it.

[117]

The Mayor sympathetically understood. He apologized for the parked car. It was altogether understandable, he continued, that such an accident should occur. He was sorry, but happy that nobody had been seriously hurt. And he wanted to take the occasion to welcome Senator Truman to Hagerstown, notwithstanding the unfortunate circumstances under which the welcome was extended. He hoped Senator Truman would come back to Hagerstown, soon and often.

In order to insure such return, would Senator Truman accept the keys to the city? The astonished Truman certainly would.

"I don't happen to have them with me at the moment," said the Mayor. "May I send them to you tomorrow? At Washington?"

That would be perfectly grand, Truman agreed.

So badly damaged was Truman's car that Vic Messall was summoned by telephone from his home near Washington.

After assuring the owner of the other car that the damage done his vehicle would be repaired, the Trumans got into Messall's car and resumed the trip to Washington.

A few days later, an expressman brought the keys to Hagerstown into Truman's office. They were, in reality, one key. It was more than a foot long, wooden, black and duly inscribed. Truman had it hung over the mantel in his outer office and kept it there until he moved to the White House.

"I'm willing to bet," he said later, "that I'm the only member of the United States Senate who has been presented with the keys of a city because he was in an automobile accident."

"It cost something, though, didn't it?" I asked.

"Plenty. Several hundred dollars for automobile repairs."

Chapter Seven

＝＊＝

ONE little day led fast to another, and almost before Harry Truman realized it five of his six senatorial years were gone. Here it was, 1940. Only yesterday, it seemed, he had learned the ropes; and now, incredibly, his term was almost over. Those days in the Senate had been happy days. He wanted more—many, many more.

There was only one way to get them, he knew, and that was to fight for them.

He would have to fight for them twice. The first fight would be for renomination, and it would be a heartbreaker. For that he would need almost everything he didn't have. It would be a sixty-day running fight, possibly longer. Over good roads and bad, under the summer's broiling sun, he would go east and west and north and south throughout Missouri. He would shake thousands of hands, make hundreds of speeches and, maybe, kiss a few dozen babies. He would spend a lot of money, to come from he knew not where.

[120]

Day after day and week after week he would have to sell himself again to the people of Missouri. That would be his job in June, July, and part of August. It would end with the primary election. Then, if he won, he would start all over again in the general election campaign to defeat the Republican nominee.

That wouldn't be bad, he thought, and it might be fun; he would rather enjoy a campaign that would bring him face to face with the homefolks again. The prize was worth the game. But before sitting in on the game, he would like to have a few chips to play with.

Where were they? He wondered. There were not many in sight; it was easier to see what he didn't have than what he had.

Tom Pendergast was serving a prison term. The organization that had given Truman the nomination in 1934 was full of fire and fight in those days; now it was supine and in disgrace. That was *his* organization, he recalled with a pang. He was still a member in good standing, still paying dues. And that, of course, would be used against him.

Maurice Milligan—ah, yes; that fellow! He was the United States District Attorney at Kansas City who had sent the Pendergast workers to jail for vote frauds. He had been in at the political death of Tom. And Milligan was saying, Truman heard, he was going to run for Truman's job, and get it.

And there was Lloyd Stark. He was the Governor, heading up the State office holders' machine, such as it was. How Truman disliked him! And what peppery letters had passed between them! Roosevelt seemed to be coddling him, making him a fair-haired boy at the White House.

Stark was going to run, too. And he talked strong, confident, and cocky.

Well, what did Truman have? What following could he command, he asked himself, to beat off Stark and Milligan?

Not money, Truman knew. He didn't have any money himself and the campaign would cost plenty.

And so long as he wasn't kidding himself, he knew he didn't have an outstanding record as Senator. No law bore his name, no great investigation. He had slaved on the Transportation Act but that was not then an act at all; it was just another bill awaiting the pleasure of Congress. In the Washington drama that had stirred the nation for those five years, he had played no heroic role.

He had been merely another New Deal senator.

But he had been a loyal New Deal senator. He had followed Roosevelt in fair weather and foul, even when grumbling he was tired of being treated like an office boy. He had voted right on every roll call except the two relating to the soldier bonus in 1936. That was a record of regularity few could match and nobody could beat. On that record he could claim the President's help.

At least he thought so. He was mistaken.

Roosevelt was running in 1940 for a third term. And he wasn't back-slapping anybody, no matter how loyal, and proclaiming jovially, "Voters, here is my choice!" He had tried it in reverse two years before, booting Democrats around and saying, "Voters, he is not my choice; retire him!" It hadn't worked so well. The voters had thrown all those candidates except one back in his teeth, electing them by thumping majorities.

Roosevelt wasn't helping anybody in the primary elections of 1940, and Harry Truman soon found it out. Suppose he had voted right for five years; what of it? Those years were a string of Yesterdays. Today was Today, and Tomorrow would be another day.

It was, "Go to it, Harry, on your own," from the White House.

For a time, Harry didn't know whether to go to it or to back away from it. He yearned for re-election, but he hesitated for weeks before deciding to go after it.

"I don't know, Bill," he told me when I asked if he were going to run again. "I'd like to come back"—a model of understatement—"but I haven't made up my mind yet."

Once when I nagged him, he asked rather crossly, "What would you do?"

"I'd make up my mind," I said.

"What do you think of my chances?"

"Not as much as I'd like to, but you do have a chance, and it easily could be made a good chance. That will depend on you. If there's anything I can do to help, I'll do it. I want you to come back, and I'll help all I can if you'll show me how."

"Suppose I don't run, or get licked. What then?"

"Then I'd get set for a good Federal job. The President would give you one, wouldn't he?"

"Maybe; what job?"

"Well, how about a place on the Interstate Commerce Commission? Seven years, ten thousand a year—not bad, eh?"

"Hmpf," he grunted. "I don't want to come back to

[123]

Washington to go on the I.C.C. I want to come back as Senator. If I can't come back as Senator, I don't want to come back at all."

"Okay, Harry. I'm for it."

"I know," he said, "but you're not very helpful."

"Sorry. I'd like to be."

His grin came back to his face. "I know you would," he said warmly, "and maybe you can be. I appreciate that. Now go away and let me figure things out."

He finally decided to ask a few close friends in Missouri to meet him at St. Louis and discuss his political course. A state-wide meeting of party workers was scheduled at the Hotel Statler there a fortnight later. Truman wrote twenty-five or thirty men of whose support he felt certain and asked them to meet with him at that time to discuss plans for his renomination.

Fewer than half showed up when he went to St. Louis and most of them were unenthusiastic. One after another, they gave reasons why they couldn't help in his primary campaign. Mayor Dickmann of St. Louis, heading the strong political machine in the city, was opposed to Truman and was supporting Stark. A cog in the machine then was an energetic young man named Hannegan. Hannegan was esteemed a natural politician by those who worked with him. He knew Truman slightly and liked him, but hesitated to oppose the organization and support him. So for the time Hannegan said nothing.

When Truman addressed the State meeting, applause was perfunctory. Such as it was, it came largely from rural delegates.

The truth came to him like a clap of thunder. All of a sudden, Harry Truman knew what he had feared to know. Lloyd Stark and Maurice Milligan were the men of the hour. The odor of the Pendergast machine clung to Truman, and the odor was bad. Among those Democrats into whose faces he looked down from the speakers' platform there was little sentiment for his candidacy and no enthusiasm.

Disillusioned and discouraged, he returned to Washington with Harry Woodring in Woodring's private plane. Woodring then was Secretary of War. Victor Messall, Truman's secretary who had gone to St. Louis with Truman, went with him to the plane.

"Come on with us, Vic, there's room for you," Woodring told Messall.

"Thank you, Mr. Secretary," Messall replied, "but I plan to go back later."

"Aren't you going with us?" Truman asked in surprise.

"No, Senator; not if it's all right with you."

"Why not, Vic?"

"Well, I want to go over to Kansas City and see Jim Pendergast. I'd like to find out what he's thinking, and whether he'll support you in the primary if you decide to run."

A day or so later Messall walked into the Pendergast organization headquarters in Kansas City. There he saw Jim Pendergast, Tom's nephew, who headed the organization Tom had directed so long.

"Jim," said Messall, "I want to ask you a question. Will you support Senator Truman if he runs for renomination?"

Jim Pendergast took the cigarette from his lips and leaned back in his chair.

"You can tell Harry Truman," he said slowly, "that if he gets only two votes in the primary one of them will be mine and the other will be my wife's."

"Thanks, Jim. That's all I want to know."

Messall telephoned Truman at Washington that afternoon, giving him Pendergast's message.

"And now, Senator," Messall went on, "if you'll send along the information I need to fill out the blank form, I'll do it and file your notice of intent to run."

To that moment Truman hadn't said Yes or No as to whether he would run again. Apparently he had not decided when Messall telephoned. There were a few moments of silence on the wire. Then Truman's voice came clear and strong to his listening secretary.

"All right, Vic; I'll do it. There's a filing fee of a hundred dollars, you know. I'll send that along by air mail, too."

"No, Senator; you don't have to do that. I've got the hundred in my pocket. You can pay me back when I return to Washington."

Messall was relieved. From the beginning he had thought Truman would run again. Now that the actual decision was made, Messall felt Truman would be renominated and re-elected. Not once in the months ahead did he waver in his belief.

Meanwhile the political wiseacres of Missouri had consigned Harry Truman to the boneyard. He was through, they were saying; done for as fully as the Pendergast machine that had sponsored him. The race was to be between

Stark and Milligan. They were the men who had killed Cock Robin. But Cock Robin wasn't dead.

Messall filed for Truman at Jefferson City the following Saturday. He waited until the Secretary of State was ready to close his office, at noon, for the week-end. Colonel Frank Erhart of Kansas City, a devoted Truman follower, was with Messall and noted the look of astonishment that spread over the Secretary's face as he read the document. The filing caused no less a sensation among the workers for Stark and Milligan.

In Washington the next week Truman and Messall took stock of prospects. These were not encouraging. They were altogether on their own resources and knew they would have to build from the ground up. Not one outstanding Democrat in the State, Jim Pendergast alone excepted, was willing at the moment to offend Stark or Milligan by avowing support for Truman.

Truman soon realized the bitter fullness of the feeling.

He decided to organize a state-wide committee to promote and finance his campaign. There were to be two chairmen, one for the eastern part of the State, the other for the western. Truman picked these men with great care. When he wrote them, both declined to serve.

He turned to Messall.

"Vic," he asked, "would you be willing to go out to Missouri and run my campaign for me?"

"Yes, Senator, I'll be very happy to—if you think I could do a good job."

"Then let's do it that way."

Messall resigned his job as Truman's secretary and hit the Missouri trail. He was to front for his friend and boss, to collect funds and run the campaign and under the Corrupt Practices Act he had to resign. There also was another law compelling him to resign. Ironically, Truman's good friend, Senator Carl Hatch of New Mexico, had sponsored the second law and it bore his name. For the period of the campaign, Messall was off the Federal pay roll. When the campaign was over, he went back to his old job.

Sedalia was selected as headquarters for the campaign committee. Messall rented a vacant old building, had essential repairs made, and moved in. Meanwhile he was telephoning over the State to Truman's friends and his own. He asked for their help; not only money but personal services. Where they had office employes who wanted to work for Truman and could be spared, Messall wanted their services as volunteers.

There was fair response to these pleas. Several old friends contributed five hundred dollars apiece, others lesser sums. Messall soon was confirming his conviction that Truman had many friends. From one in St. Louis came generous aid in providing office space for the committee's big branch there. Before long, many volunteers were donating their services.

A campaign committee was set up. Its name was a jawbreaker: "The Harry S. Truman for U. S. Senator Renomination and Election Committee." Messall was Chairman and "Millie" Dryden was Secretary.

"Millie," as she was known to hundreds on Capitol Hill in Washington, was Mrs. Mildred L. Dryden. She hailed from Truman's home town of Independence and had been his secretary when he was a "Judge" on the Jackson County

Board of Commissioners. When he became senator she went to Washington, wrote his confidential letters and became his receptionist. She was deft and efficient and soon became popular on Capitol Hill.

In 1940 she went back to her home state to work long hours for Truman in his campaign.

The new committee had eleven vice chairmen and an advisory board. Almost everybody was made happy with an imposing title. The board was headed by a Springfield lawyer, Sam Wear. It took nerve to accept the responsibility and brave the wrath of Stark and Milligan. Wear wasn't afraid of those two; he worked full time for Truman.

Five years later, Wear's loaf was cast up by the waters. President Truman nominated him to be United States Attorney at Kansas City to succeed Maurice Milligan.

Another vice chairman was Frank Lee of Joplin. Lee had been in Congress and Messall had been his secretary. Philip Welch, Mayor of St. Joseph, was a third vice chairman. Others included John Farrington of Springfield, James R. Wade of Sullivan, D. C. Campbell of Maysville, Dr. W. L. Brandon of Poplar Bluff, Delmar Dail of Marceline, Phil Groves of Neosho, Sterling McCarty of Caruthersville, Frank Monroe of Sedalia, and Mortimer Levy of Moberly.

Not all were experienced campaigners, but some of them were and all were strong for Truman and enthusiastic. When Stark and Milligan leaders read the listing they smiled; "half of them a bunch of amateurs," they said, not knowing any more about politics than the man they were working for. The "amateurs" were showing their mettle, however, before the campaign swung into the homestretch.

[129]

Roger Sermon, Mayor of Independence and Truman's old-time friend, was appointed Chairman of the Finance Committee. Mayor Sermon was not a man of large means; he contributed both time and money to the campaign.

Truman's friends and fortunes were perking up. Messall, who seemed to be everywhere at once and always cocksure of the result, stimulated the workers. Truman himself kept them in good humor and inspired them. The little coterie running his campaign knew him well and knew he wasn't involved in the dirty work that had wrecked the Pendergast machine. Because of their conviction, they worked the harder to vindicate him.

Harry Vaughan of St. Louis was appointed Treasurer of the committee. Vaughan at that time was a Lieutenant Colonel in the Army Reserve Corps. He and Truman had become friends a dozen years before through their common interest in veterans' affairs.

Divisions were set up in the committee. Mrs. Henry Clay Chiles of Lexington headed the Women's Division. J. V. Conran of New Madrid was appointed Chairman of the Speakers' Division. A newspaper publisher at Sikeston, W. L. Blanton, Sr., headed the Publicity Committee. Tom Evans of Kansas City took over the Chairmanship of the Radio Division. Tom Van Sant of Fulton was appointed Chairman of the Budget Committee, and Roy Harper of Caruthersville headed the State Offices Committee.

Their names, with others, were strung down the left margin of a letterhead printed in red, white, and blue, and graced with the candidate's picture in the upper right-hand corner. As a work of art, the letterhead was pronounced second only to the tongue-twisting name given the campaign committee.

It was no great shakes of a showing, but it was pretty good, at that, Truman felt, and certainly it was the best that could be put together in a hurry. A few of the names were known fairly well throughout the State. Most were known locally and each had a following in his own community.

With the campaign committee organized and ready for work, Truman looked over the field again. Where would he get the votes he needed, and where would he get the money to run the campaign?

He was willing to go in debt again, and that is what he did to the extent of several thousand dollars. But that would supply only a part of the needed funds; he would have to look elsewhere for the rest. As for votes, he knew better where he wouldn't get them than where he would.

He wouldn't get many, for instance, in St. Louis where the city machine was hot for Stark. Unless something akin to a miracle should happen there, he feared, he wouldn't carry the city.

Nor could he count on a big vote in many of the other cities. Practically every daily newspaper in Missouri opposed him. One, the Kansas City *Journal*, successor to the *Journal-Post*, was blatantly supporting him. Some of the weekly newspapers in rural regions supported him, declaring he was upright and able despite his former close association with the Pendergast machine. These expressions encouraged him to court the farm vote.

He didn't have to dress up his voting record in the

Senate to go courting there. With farm subsidies, soil conservation, every other Roosevelt panacea for farm ills, Truman had gone along one hundred per cent. His record, he felt, should entitle him to strong support in the country sections where the Federal funds had been distributed. He was right.

Organized Labor—there was where he ought to get his big vote! Well did Truman realize it. But in that field he was handicapped a bit. He was identified chiefly with the rail labor unions, rather than the big A. F. of L. and the C. I. O. Some of the rail union heads were his buddies and all were his friends. So was all rail labor; a photograph circulated among the state's newspapers showed forty-two persons, rail workers and their wives, standing before a locomotive—all of one family and all for Truman.

If the rail workers could influence other unions in Truman's behalf, a huge block of votes would be cast for him. Certainly the idea was worth following up; and the Truman workers did follow it up handsomely.

The biggest rail labor union of them all was the Brotherhood of Railway Trainmen, and its President, A. F. "Aleck" Whitney, knew Truman and liked him. Whitney went to work in Truman's behalf quickly and effectively; he was among those who regarded Truman as one of the best friends Labor ever had in the Senate. Another rail labor chieftain who did not know Truman as well as Whitney did was Alvaney Johnston of the Brotherhood of Locomotive Engineers. Johnston supported Truman. So did other rail labor groups.

Whitney's organization had political workers with know-how, and it had barrels of money. Several of its top-flight officials were sent into Missouri by Whitney to help Truman in his primary campaign. Those Paul Reveres of the the rail brotherhoods rode the highways and byways for weeks, calling on all union men in the State to rally under the Truman standard. They helped save the day for him.

Their services were donated, costing Truman nothing. Nor was that the full measure of the donation. With other rail labor unions, the trainmen published a weekly newspaper at Washington, *Labor.* A special edition was printed for the Missouri campaign. It was devoted wholly to proclaiming what a good friend the working classes of the nation had in Harry Truman. Five hundred thousand copies of this edition were sent into the State, blanketing all labor unions.

This was done at a moment when Truman's fortunes were flagging. The effect was tonic, and the cost to Truman was nothing.

Nor did the Whitney union stop there.

In its need for money, the Truman committee was enrolling members at a dollar a head. Or, rather, it was trying to do so. Booklets containing ten blank Certificates of Membership were printed and sent to committee workers throughout the State. Each worker was requested to enroll ten new members and send the ten dollars in dues to the committee.

The idea didn't work well; Missouri voters showed stiff sales resistance. When the plan was failing, the driving forces of the rail labor unions came to its rescue. They bought the little booklets by the hundreds and chuted thousands of dollars into the campaign where it would do the most good.

These great exertions by the rail labor unions to renominate Harry Truman may have caused some of the leaders to feel that Truman owed them something in return. If so, that feeling was never expressed. It may be that some of them felt they were not only rewarding "one of the best friends Labor ever had in the Senate" for past services to the cause of Labor, but reasonably could look forward to gratifying returns in the future. If so, they had a rude awakening six years later.

That was in the spring of 1946. Harry Truman was Senator from Missouri no longer; he was President of the United States. A strike of railway trainmen and locomotive engineers had been called and was about to be made effective with paralyzing results on the nation's affairs. President Truman went to the Capitol and addressed Congress, asking for drastic legislation to break the threatened strikes.

"This particular crisis," Truman told Congress, "has been brought about by the obstinate arrogance of two men. They are Mr. Alvaney Johnston, President of the Brotherhood of Locomotive Engineers, and Mr. A. F. Whitney, President of the Brotherhood of Railway Trainmen. Eighteen other unions and all of the railroad companies are ready to run the railroads. These two men have tried to stop them."

No such development as that could possibly be foreseen in 1940 when Whitney, Johnston, and others were seeing to it that Harry Truman was renominated Senator.

Another large group from whom Truman thought he

should poll many votes in the campaign of 1940 was the veterans of the First World War. A division of the committee to cultivate the veterans was set up under the chairmanship of P. L. Shackleford of Moberly.

Two other groups were courted by the committee. One was composed of the considerable number of Jewish voters in the towns and cities. A Zionist, David Berenstein of St. Louis, was given a high place in the committee. The second group was the Negroes.

There were tens of thousands of Negro voters in Missouri. Truman and his workers assiduously went after their votes. A Negro division was set up in the committee. At its head was placed one of the most prominent Negroes in the nation. This was Dr. William J. Thompkins of Kansas City who had been appointed by Roosevelt as Register of Deeds for the District of Columbia.

Truman appealed from the stump for the Negro vote. In so doing he not only followed Roosevelt's lead but observed the custom set by other Democratic candidates in every section of the country except the Southern States.

One of the meetings Truman addressed was held by the National Colored Democratic Association in the Eighth Regiment Armory at Chicago on July 14, 1940. Eight or nine speakers, fairly evenly divided between whites and Negroes, addressed the meeting. Among the white speakers, along with Truman, were Senators Barkley of Kentucky, the Majority Leader in the upper House, Guffey of Pennsylvania, and Minton of Indiana.

Truman's brief address to the Negroes was inserted, as were the other addresses, in the *Congressional Record* by

[135]

Senator Schwellenbach of Washington not long thereafter. Publication in the *Record* resulted in its receiving the franking privilege through the mails.

In his address, Truman said:

"I wish to make it clear that I am not appealing for social equality of the Negro. The Negro himself knows better than that, and the highest type of Negro leaders say quite frankly they prefer the society of their own people. Negroes want justice, not social relations.

"I merely wish to sound a note of warning. Numberless antagonisms and indignities heaped upon any race will eventually try human patience to the limit and a crisis will develop. We all know that the Negro is here to stay and in no way can be removed from our political and economic life, and we should recognize his inalienable rights as specified in our Constitution. Can any man claim protection of our laws if he denies that protection to others?

"Under the Roosevelt Administration more has been done to give the Negro equal legal, economic and cultural rights than has ever been done before. The Honorable John M. Houston of Kansas has said that President Roosevelt has appointed more Negroes to responsible governmental positions than the last three Republican Administrations combined. While these are individual honors, the colored people will benefit by the Roosevelt policies.

"Every law passed by our present Congress for direct relief or otherwise gives the Negro his equal rights.

"For the first time in our history, the Administration has given us a colored man in the White House on the secretarial staff. . . ."

Truman did not wait until July to appeal for the Negro

vote, nor did he defer the appeal until he was out of the state. On the opening day of his primary campaign at Sedalia, June 15, he said:

"I believe in the brotherhood of man, not merely the brotherhood of white men but the brotherhood of all men before law.

"I believe in the Constitution and the Declaration of Independence. In giving the Negroes the rights which are theirs we are only acting in accord with our ideals of a true democracy.

"If any class or race can be permanently set apart from, or pushed down below, the rest in political and civil rights, so may any other class or race when it shall incur the displeasure of its more powerful associates, and we may say farewell to the principles on which we count our safety.

"In the years past, lynching and mob violence, lack of schools, and countless other unfair conditions hastened the progress of the Negro from the country to the city. In these centers the Negroes never had much chance in regard to work or anything else. By and large they went to work mainly as unskilled laborers and domestic servants.

"They have been forced to live in segregated slums, neglected by the authorities. Negroes have been preyed upon by all types of exploiters from the installment salesmen of clothing, pianos, and furniture to the vendors of vice.

"The majority of our Negro people find but cold comfort in shanties and tenements. Surely, as freemen, they are entitled to something better than this. . . . It is our duty to see that the Negroes in our locality have increased opportunity to exercise their privilege as freemen. . . ."

[137]

The campaign now was rolling. In opening it at Sedalia, Truman was joined by two of his senatorial buddies, Hatch of New Mexico and Schwellenbach. Later in the campaign Senator Barkley spoke in Truman's behalf at St. Louis. Other New Deal senators were desired as speakers but most of them were busy with their own campaigns.

Missouri's interest was divided somewhat between the primary election campaign, which sizzled from its start, and the war in Europe as well as our own newly inaugurated national defense program.

Not even the red fire and brass bands of the political campaign could crowd from the spotlight Hitler's sensational sweep through the Low Countries, Italy's entrance into the conflict, and the fall of France. And there was feverish interest in the formation of the defense program.

Somewhat earlier, Truman had been a member of a committee of senators and representatives that toured army posts in the United States and inspected American defenses in Panama and Puerto Rico.

"I believe," he told a radio audience from Station KMOX at St. Louis on June 30, "that an army of 400,000 men is adequate for the first line of defense on land and to act as instructors to the citizen army.

"I think we should have a navy second to none and the necessary air force to support it. If it takes 50,000 planes and 100,000 pilots, let's build the planes and train the pilots.

"I think we should have a citizen army trained on the Swiss plan, subject to call in case of emergency, and the necessary tanks, armament, and other matériel to equip those forces. . . .

"I personally do not believe that we will or should become involved in the European brawl. I do believe, however, that we should be prepared to defend the Monroe Doctrine and the Western Hemisphere, and that we ought to sell all the planes and matériel possible to the British Empire. . . .

"There is another phase of national defense which is of vital interest to our country and its welfare. That is the disloyal inhabitants who are enjoying peace and freedom here and yet who would like to overthrow our form of government.

"I believe that these people should be sent to the countries they admire and that every effort should be made to eliminate any fifth-column activities. That is being done by the proper authorities. But we must not become hysterical and go witch-hunting in our enthusiasm to eliminate a possible fifth column."

Truman's chances for winning rose with such speeches. The people of Missouri lapped up what he had to say about the national defense. He then was a member of the Senate Committee on Military Affairs with direct supervision over the Army and familiar with its secrets and plans. His prediction that the United States would not become involved in "the European brawl" soured to whey in little more than a year, but when he made it he spoke the thought of virtually all his committee colleagues and millions of Americans.

Day by day as he toured the state, making from three to five speeches every twenty-four hours, his popularity increased. The prospect was changing. When the three-man contest opened, it was the general belief in the state that

Stark and Milligan would dwarf Truman and leave him trailing far behind.

Another of the numerous breaks that came Truman's way occurred to upset this prospect altogether on the day Milligan made the first speech of his campaign.

In that first address to the voters, Milligan sounded the knell of his own hopes. He made a poor impression. Not only did he handle himself awkwardly, but he was inept in some of his utterances and unfortunate in his manner of delivery. It was apparent in the first few minutes that Milligan had a poorly prepared speech and that he was no orator.

The crowd that came to whoop for him didn't whoop. Before he had finished his address, they were dribbling away. They had enough. His friends realized then that he couldn't win. He stayed in the race, but it narrowed at once to Stark and Truman. In its early stages, Stark was far out in the lead. Truman came up fast behind him and as they neared the homestretch they were running neck and neck.

Bennett Clark helped start the real swing to Truman.

Clark had been on the sidelines, noncommittal. He had been Milligan's first sponsor; in the early days of the New Deal, Roosevelt had made Milligan the United States Attorney at Kansas City on Clark's recommendation. That was before Truman became senator.

When it became obvious, in 1940, that Milligan couldn't win the nomination as senator, Clark decided something ought to be done to prevent Stark from winning. Clark didn't relish the idea of having fruit-grower Stark, with untold baskets of apples to give away, as his colleague in

the Senate. Harry Truman had no apples or anything else
to give away. He was preferable to Stark, as Clark saw it
then, yet Clark and Truman were not intimate friends.

"Why should I do anything to help Harry Truman get
renominated?" Clark asked Messall during the 1940 campaign when Messall appealed to him for support. "Truman
never did anything to help me in my campaign" (1938).

"You're mistaken, Senator," Messall replied. "He made
two speeches for you in that campaign."

"When? Where?"

"I ought to know, but I can't give you exact dates and
places now," Messall said. "I'll look it up. But I know I'm
right."

"No, Vic; you're wrong."

The conference lasted two hours and Messall got nowhere. When Messall went back to his hotel, he saw Senator Hatch in the lobby.

"What's the matter, Vic?" Hatch asked. "You look as if
you were all in."

"I've been trying to get Senator Clark to come out to
Missouri and make a few speeches for Truman. And I can't
even get him to say he'll support Truman."

"What!" exclaimed Hatch. "Bennett not going to support Harry Truman? Why, that's—where is Bennett now?"

"At his office, I suppose. I left him there a few minutes
ago."

Hatch stepped into a public telephone booth. Leaving
the door ajar, he motioned to Messall.

"What's this I hear?" Hatch asked when Clark came on
the wire. "I mean about your not supporting Harry Truman."

After listening a few moments to what Clark said, Hatch interrupted.

"I'm coming over now to your office," he said. "Wait for me."

A few days later Clark went to St. Louis. From his rooms in the Mayfair Hotel he telephoned his political lieutenants throughout Missouri. The burden of his instructions was that they should get ready to support Truman. Ten days or so thereafter, Clark made a public announcement of his support for Truman. Thereafter he campaigned in Truman's behalf.

Clark was far back in Roosevelt's doghouse then because of his earlier fight against the court-packing and reorganization programs. Truman had supported both of these. Despite White House ill favor, Clark still was a political power in his own state.

His move evoked no cheers at the White House. Stark had been a frequent visitor there. Roosevelt had taken him down the Potomac on the Presidential yacht, and Stark had been mentioned as a possible successor to the ailing Claude Swanson, Secretary of the Navy. Truman workers didn't care for that; they suspected that Roosevelt preferred Stark to Truman in the Senate. Some of them, but not Truman himself, grumbled that the President ought to keep his hands off the red-hot contest in Missouri; that if he couldn't endorse a senator who had supported him in everything he proposed, he at least shouldn't openly show favors to the senator's opponent. This talk, however, came to nothing.

In the final days of the primary campaign—within a week before its close—Truman got another break that really was magnificent: Bob Hannegan crashed into the picture.

He did so with an explosion that practically blew the Stark forces into the next county.

A minor cog in the St. Louis machine, and as shrewd and calculating a politician as a tough ward ever produced, Hannegan had gone along loyally with his organization for Stark. But he didn't like the notion; he had an idea that Stark was going to lose, and he wanted to get on the bandwagon. The more he thought about the prospect, the likelier this seemed; and the likelier this seemed, the more he got fed up on the Stark candidacy. The nearer the election, the fuller he became.

One fine day in the homestretch, Bob Hannegan had enough. He told the machine where it could go, declared he was for Harry Truman and went feverishly to work for his new allegiance. As one of the leaders in a St. Louis ward, he knew better than a thousand lay voters the full worth of organization. And he had the knack of organizing.

He knew some other leaders who wanted to get over on the winning side, and these were fed up, too. When he called for help to nominate Truman, help answered by the automobile load.

Bob Hannegan took command and issued his orders. By day and night as the few remaining hours ticked off he and his crowd rang doorbells and telephones, buttonholed voters and lined them up for Truman. The machine was hit so hard and unexpectedly by this indefatigable young man and his crew that before it could recover from its confusion, primary day had come and gone.

St. Louis plumped into the Truman column. A miracle had been needed and Bob Hannegan had wrought the miracle.

"He did it—and how!" Messall said. "He was responsible for Truman's winning in St. Louis."

The miracle paid off handsomely. In less than six years Bob Hannegan the unknown became successively the Collector of Internal Revenue at St. Louis, the Commissioner of Internal Revenue with headquarters at Washington, the Chairman of the Democratic National Committee, and the Postmaster General in Harry Truman's Cabinet. He also became the presiding genius of Truman's political strategy for 1948.

Throughout the bitter primary campaign of 1940, Truman had taken it on the chin. Again and again, Stark and Milligan linked him in terms almost insulting with the old Pendergast machine. Not once in the long, fiery fight did Truman utter an unkind syllable about his old friend, Tom Pendergast.

Yes, Truman not only admitted but proclaimed, he had been Tom's friend and he wasn't ashamed of it. Since when had friendship become a crime?

Yes, he was loyal to his friends, all of them. He was not "a rat to desert a sinking ship." That was plain talk and it hit the hearts of the plain people to whom it was addressed. The voters who had been apathetic at first soon were flocking to hear him. And when Stark and Milligan workers tried to make capital of his reference to a rat on a sinking ship, it reacted and made more votes for Truman.

"Good old Harry!" the voters yelled. "True to his friends even when they go to jail!"

A fortnight before primary election day the state was seething. The fight was furious and at close quarters. Even a blind man could see that the fighters were evenly matched, could sense a photo finish. It was Stark and Truman then, all the way to the last climactic moment. Yet Milligan lingered on with his effort and by doing so undoubtedly contributed to the success of the man he bitterly sought to defeat.

When the votes were counted, Truman had won. His plurality was something to look at under a microscope—approximately 8,300 votes.

Had 4,200 of Missouri's sons and daughters switched that day from Truman to Stark, another man would be in the White House now. The pipsqueak margin decided the identity of the thirty-third President of the United States.

It was given to a man who had been given many another break over a lucky decade. Some of them had been skin-of-the-teeth breaks. Others still lay hidden in Fortune's kit, to come to him. Each pushed him a little closer to the Presidency. Each was a break he had to have to get there. And few were closer than his 8,300-vote margin over Stark, stretching across Missouri from the fastnesses of the Ozarks to the rolling Mississippi.

Chapter Eight

===========*===========

ONCE more Harry Truman was the Democratic nominee for Senator from Missouri. His grilling primary campaign was behind him. Ahead lay the campaign for re-election. The toughest part of his political return to Washington was over. Now the professional politicians of the State Democratic Committee would have charge of his election. They would assume such worries as he had carried in the primary fight. They would raise money, arrange for speakers, buy radio time, pay bills, and attend to all the rest of it.

The price tag on his nomination was more than twenty-one thousand dollars; to be exact, $21,573.76. Truman had the accounting done in Missouri and filed the figures, as required by law, with the Secretary of the Senate at Washington.

He had spent more than his friends contributed. His statement disclosed that $20,750.78 had been donated and that the cost of soliciting those donations—telephone

ent best within him. And he would serve the whole country better, if he could, in his second term than in his first. He would rise above the level of partisan politics. He would be a senator in the Missouri tradition, so help him God, if that were in his power. He thought it was.

When Harry Truman took the Senate's oath for the second time the country was preparing for war. The National Guard had been called to the colors. At a dollar a year or W.O.C. (Without Compensation), industrial and labor leaders were flocking to Washington to draw the blueprints for the coming conflict. The Government was recruiting tens of thousands of civilian workers monthly. Billions of make-ready funds were rolling from the Treasury.

In great haste, attended by much waste and confusion, army camps and munition plants were springing up all over the country. The Navy had started building the greatest fleet. Airplane plants were expanding overnight. Ten years of hard times were retreating before the greatest wartime boom in history.

Four little weasel words sugar-coated the mammoth effort: "For the national defense." As the nation was nominally at peace, the warlike plans probably had to be called that or something like it. But Truman wasn't fooled. He had fought in the First World War. Under the sugar-coating phrase he saw the bitter medicine and knew it for what it was.

What he saw distressed and angered him.

Among other things, he saw a Labor clique and a Capital clique, each greedily pawing for spoils. Small production plants by the hundreds were eager to help make war matériel—scores of them were in his own state. Truman saw those plants shunted aside and hogtied to inactivity by grasping Big Business intent on getting while the getting was good.

Dominant Big Business had made Little Business impotent for war production, as Truman saw the scene, in the name of the Government itself. That had been done through the power to make decisions for the Government which had been given dollar-a-year men and W.O.C. industrialists directing the program at Washington.

As for Labor, workers by the tens of thousands were eager for employment opened by the mammoth program. Truman saw those workers denied jobs unless they first paid for the privilege of working, with so-called initiation fees to local unions. That, he soon learned, was regarded as quite proper by the high Labor officials bedded down comfortably at a dollar-a-year or W.O.C.

Looking closer, he saw Capital demand and get from the Government tax concessions that made scot-free presents to great corporations of war production plants over a five-year period. And he saw Labor demand and get Government approval of swollen wages and union membership requirements that barred independent workers from any participation in the program unless they complied with the harsh requirements.

The one was Labor's price for its contribution to the national defense program, the other was Capital's. Capital and Labor were riding the gravy train in those days of national peril and each had its own engineer at the throttle.

What Harry Truman saw stirred his indignation to its depths. He longed angrily to end the saturnalia of greed.

"I'm utterly disgusted," he told me early in January, 1941. "I simply can't subscribe to the bungling and waste that crop up everywhere. I can't stomach the grasping greed of Big Business or the cunning greed of some of these labor unions."

He was sitting at the desk of his inner office and I was in a chair nearby. He paused a few moments, looked down, and then up into my eyes.

"There's too much here that's wrong," he went on. "I think I'll have to make a speech in the Senate about it."

"That would be a helpful move," I agreed. "You could make a very effective speech. You would make the first pages of the newspapers if you did, and it might do a little good."

He shot me a quick, surprised glance.

"Yes, I think it would," he said.

"I'm just wondering, Harry, if that is the answer," I went on. "You would call attention to a lot of things most folks already know about in a vague sort of way. You would get commendatory editorials and for a few days your speech would be a live subject. Then it would be forgotten, and things probably would rock along just as they are rocking now. Don't you think so?"

"It might be just that way," he said.

"You want to put an end to these conditions, don't you?"

"Of course."

"Then why in the hell don't you *do* something to end them instead of getting up on your hind legs in the Senate and making another speech?"

My vehemence jarred him. He leaned forward, all attention.

[151]

"What, for instance?" he asked.

"Why don't you call for a committee to investigate this rotten situation? That would be doing something besides just making a speech, wouldn't it?"

"It surely would," he said eagerly.

"You, of course, would head that committee; you'd be its chairman. You'd have the power of the United States Senate behind you. You could go anywhere, examine anything. You could turn such a live-wire current of publicity on these bastards that they'd be running for cover when they saw you coming."

He slapped his hand down hard on my knee, got up from his seat and pounded my arm.

"You're right, Bill!" he exclaimed. "You're absolutely right. I *will* do something about it. I'm going to do just what you've suggested!"

And he did. The decision was to lift him from the ruck of the Senate and make him outstanding. It was eventually to win the Vice Presidency for him. Many a time thereafter he reminded me of that interview, telling me he wanted to repay me for the idea and if there were anything he could do for me to be sure to let him know about it. And once before a dozen or so of my Press Gallery colleagues he was so kind as to bring up the subject himself and proclaim that "Bill Helm started my investigation of the defense program."

All of which was inborn in Harry Truman and endeared him to those with whom he came in contact.

Having adopted the idea fervently, he discussed it first with some of his cronies and then with the Senate leaders. The New Deal coterie that ran the Senate were amazed.

They had investigated financiers, industrialists, banks, railroads and public utilities, but never any of their own agencies. The idea was altogether new and a bit shocking, in a way. It was something to be mulled over; it could lead here but it might lead there. Such an investigation might forestall a scandal after the passing of the crisis. Or it might publicize so much rottenness that the country would turn against the Administration.

And Harry Truman, of all people, to be the investigator! It really didn't add up right. What they didn't know, and therefore couldn't understand, was the change in Harry Truman's heart. When you looked at him and talked with him, he hadn't changed a bit. He was just as good a mixer, just as regular a Party voter, as ever. Yet here he was with a proposition to investigate the Administration which, of course, was the same thing as investigating himself.

They wanted to know more about the business. Truman told them. He wasn't going on a witch hunt. He had just been re-elected, and he didn't need publicity. But couldn't they see some things were going badly? Didn't they want to do something to improve conditions? Wouldn't it be better to look into the matter now, themselves, than to leave it to possibly hostile investigators years later?

The answer was a doubting "Maybe." For several weeks the idea was batted back and forth in cloakrooms and informal talks among the leaders. Some wondered if he simply wanted to be chairman of a committee. Well, he could have that, but they'd tie his hands. And if he secretly were planning a little reform job, they'd give him a committee that would tie his hands.

They trusted him; Oh, yes! Implicitly, or eighty per cent

implicitly. But as cagey old politicians they knew one could never tell what might happen.

Truman waited until he had won the leaders over, and then wrote his resolution with great pains. On February 10, 1941, he made his speech and sent his resolution to the desk. It called for a committee of five senators to investigate the conduct of the defense program with a grant of $25,000 for expenses. A provision was included under which the committee could call on downtown agencies for clerical and professional help.

It was a deft and carefully prepared appeal. Not only did Truman cite instances of abuses; he reminded his colleagues that the omnipotents downtown who were running the program didn't hesitate to brush off senators when the latter came along with helpful little suggestions, such as, "How about giving my constituent here, Jim Jones, a big Government contract?"

Most of the Senate's membership had delusions as to their own importance when they asked such questions. They didn't care for the deflation they suffered.

Truman reminded the Senate of the three-man advisory board to the War Department. He didn't have to do that; most of his colleagues already were aware of the pain in the neck resulting from bumping into the board. Contracts were awarded nominally by the Secretary of War, but as he invariably followed the advice of the board, the latter effectively had the say as to who got contracts and who didn't. Truman unearthed instances where big awards had been made to firms officered by acquaintances or friends of the board's members rather than to senators' constituents.

It was a good talking point for his resolution.

"This [friendship], however should not effect any criticism," he said. "Friends may have been made because of their quality performance. Friendship should not be a handicap to anyone seeking work in the War Department.

"When a friendship, however, dominates the selection of a contractor, then that is wrong."

He had the Senate's rapt attention now. Leaving the theme momentarily he discussed the concentration of plants given Government contracts. These were largely in the industrial centers of the East and the Midwest into neither of which Missouri seemed to fit. Then he came back quickly to the sore spot.

"It is considered a sin," he continued, "for a United States Senator to make a recommendation for contractors, although we may be more familiar with the efficiency and ability of our contractors than anybody in the War Department."

Nor did he overlook the opportunity to throw a few stones at Big Business. One organization, which he named, had received from $300,000,000 to $500,000,000 in engineering and architectural contracts, he asserted. This was at a time when his own efforts to get some of this business awarded to firms in Missouri had been a washout.

"I am calling the attention of the Senate to these things," he concluded, "because I believe most sincerely that they need looking into.

"I am particularly alarmed at the concentration of these national defense industrial plants. I am reliably informed that from seventy to ninety per cent of the contracts let have been concentrated in an area smaller than England.

It undoubtedly is the plan to make the big manufacturers bigger and let the little men shift for themselves.

"I am merely saying what I believe to be conditions that deserve investigation. If nothing is wrong, then there will be no harm done. If it is wrong, it ought to brought to light."

Vice President Wallace referred Truman's resolution to the Committee on Contingent Expenses, the so-called purse-strings committee. It was the customary reference for a measure calling for a Senate investigation that would cost money. One of the committee's functions was to recommend the size of the dollar grant for carrying on the work.

James F. ("Jimmy") Byrnes of South Carolina was Chairman. Senator Byrnes was popular, but he had a reputation for tightness in recommending funds for investigations. He and Truman were not intimate at that time and their relations were rather casual. Byrnes thought Truman wanted too much money for his committee.

Instead of $25,000, about $10,000 would be all the committee needed to start, Byrnes thought. Nuts to that, Truman replied in substance; the committee really needed more than $25,000 and just put that figure in to be economical. A week of friendly deadlock ensued. Presently Truman said he wouldn't be fussy; he would settle for $20,-000.

"Too much," Byrnes replied. "Twice as much as you need."

After more friendly haggling they split the difference. Byrnes agreed to recommend $15,000 which probably was the sum he had had in mind from the beginning.

Before recommending that the Senate grant the committee $15,000, Byrnes changed Truman's resolution. Byrnes had led the New Deal forces in the Senate fight to pass Roosevelt's reorganization bill and had seen many a New Dealer run off the reservation then. He wasn't taking any chances on the new committee. Truman had wanted five senators on the committee; Byrnes made the number seven. And where Truman had planned for the membership to be made up of two Republicans and three Democrats, Byrnes made it two Republicans and five Democrats.

The Byrnes report was made to the Senate late in the afternoon of Saturday, March 1. The day had been long and tiring and was the close of a long and tiring week. There were only sixteen senators on the floor at the time. None objected when Byrnes moved suspension of the rules and adoption of the resolution.

By unanimous consent the motion prevailed and the Special Committee to Investigate the National Defense Program was authorized.

The next step was the appointment of the committee. As author of the resolution, Truman was entitled to the chairmanship. Selection of the other members nominally was to be made by Vice President Wallace. Actually, they were selected at informal conferences among Wallace, Truman, Barkley, and McNary who was Minority Leader. Presumably the President was consulted as well.

The leaders still weren't taking any chances with the senator who had sent word to the President he was tired of being treated like an office boy. They knew Truman was a good fellow who had followed leadership on practically every roll call, and they thought he would conduct his new committee work pleasantly and decently without any monkey business. But insurance was insurance, and everybody, including the Administration, ought to carry at least a little.

So they decided to put only simon-pure, tried and tested New Dealers on the committee as his Democratic associates. They suggested various names to Truman, and he didn't like some of them.

"They want to put Senator ———— on my committee," he told me. "I don't wan't him; he's an old fuddy-duddy. And they suggested Old ———— who would be of no earthly use to the rest of us. Then they wanted to know how I felt about ————. I told them No. He's a stuffed shirt."

Wallace and Barkley kept those candidates off the listing. But they didn't swerve in the slightest from their intention to take out an insurance policy against irregularity. They named four one hundred per cent New Dealers. Two were Truman's senatorial cronies and the other two were his friends although not his cronies. The Republicans selected their two members from a group reckoned reasonably decent toward the New Deal.

One of the original Republicans mentioned for a place was Tobey, but at Truman's objection his name was withdrawn.

When agreement was reached, Wallace named the members of the committee. Truman was Chairman and the others were:

Democrat Tom Connally of Texas, no Truman intimate although Truman was fond of him; a model of party regularity.

Democrat Carl Hatch of New Mexico, Truman's close friend; New Dealer from skin to core.

Democrat James Mead of New York, not in Truman's immediate orbit; willing to lay down his political life—which he later did—for the dear old New Deal.

Democrat Mon Wallgren of Washington, new to the Senate, for whom Truman conceived great liking; didn't vote wrong once during his senatorial term.

Republican Joseph Ball of Minnesota, party irregular who supported Roosevelt for President in 1944.

Republican Owen Brewster of Maine, seldom very impolite when he disagreed with the New Deal.

I wondered what Roosevelt thought of the idea and of the committee, so one day I asked him. The question was put at a White House press conference. Mr. Roosevelt said he favored the investigation and hoped it would be thorough. It was the least he could have said in its favor.

Thus equipped with a left-handed blessing from the White House, with $15,000 of the Senate's cash to draw on, and with a New Deal-packed committee, Harry Truman was ready to start on his inquiry into the defense program.

It would be one of those here-today-and-gone-tomorrow things, the Senate leaders felt. Harry and his boys might throw stones at dollar-a-year men, W.O.C.'s, generals, admirals, and a tough labor leader or two; but nobody really rating among New Deal regulars had anything to fear.

Chairman Truman had other ideas, decidedly. He wasn't gunning for any individual, he wasn't looking for scandal, and he didn't give a damn about personal glorification. But he definitely intended to find out, if he could, what was wrong with the lumbering, tardy, wasteful program. And he was going to tell the world what he found. He was looking for no fight. But he was looking for facts regardless of their environment—even if they should be hiding under the President's desk.

"The first thing I've got to do," he told me, "is to get a full-time, Number One lawyer to carry on this investigation under the committee's direction.

"This investigation is going to be important enough to call for such a man. I'm going to see Bob Jackson and get him to give us his best man. He'll grumble like the devil, I have no doubt, but I think he'll come through. He's my good friend."

Bob Jackson was Robert H. Jackson, the Attorney General. Later Mr. Jackson became an Associate Justice of the Supreme Court of the United States.

"Another thing," Truman continued, "we're not going to conduct our investigation on a political basis—not while I'm Chairman. There'll be no witch-hunting, and there'll be no whitewashing, either."

Truman sold the idea to his fellow committeemen at their first meeting. They gave him free hand to hire the ringmaster. And they agreed that politics should stop at the closed door behind which they decided policies.

For the forty-month period of Truman's chairmanship they kept their agreement. Some of them dropped out and were replaced during the period, and the membership was expanded to eleven as the scope of the inquiry broadened. Pressures were applied to all: To go easy about investigating this or that situation, and to refrain entirely from investigating other situations. These attempts failed;

all the pressure groups got for their work was the exercise involved.

It was quite unusual for a congressional committee to adopt such a policy. Soon an even more unusual condition became apparent: The committee's reports invariably were unanimous. With the Senate's best mixer in the chair, there were no backbiting and no cliques. There were differences of opinion, to be sure; and sometimes some of the members were peeved a bit by the attitude and actions of their General Counsel. But Truman quickly smoothed back ruffling feathers. The committee was one of the most harmonious and happiest in either House.

As General Counsel, Truman wanted a vigorous young man with a prosecuting attorney's complex. In earlier days when he was puncturing the bubbles of rail financiers he had found such a man in Max Lowenthal. The rail inquiry had perched fairly often on first pages of the newspapers, even in competition with early developments in the European war. That good publicity helped carry the Transportation Act to the statute books.

Now Truman wanted publicity that would write something no less important, if there should be found need therefor, on the statute books. He didn't know whether there would be need for legislation; with proper publicity there might not be. He wanted the services of a man who knew how to run a Grade A congressional investigation and such men were as rare as triplets.

Byrnes hadn't given Truman much leeway for hiring a genius. Pay would have to be mostly in glory. The fifteen thousand dollars Byrnes recommended would have to pay salaries of all workers except those on downtown pay rolls who might be loaned temporarily to the committee. That was a comforting arrangement: The committee would get the service and the downtown agencies would continue the workers on their pay rolls. Senate committees used it on a big scale.

A rich vein of talent could be tapped without cost to the committee under that arrangement. Auditors, examiners, accountants, lawyers and trained investigators were blooming in attractive bouquets on half a dozen downtown boards and commissions. They were not easy to pluck, Truman found; the agencies had a defensive way of screening their best from congressional raiding and generally displaying the culls. But Truman hadn't come to Washington the night before. He knew his way around. Before the agencies could set up their screens he captured some of their good men and took them to Capitol Hill.

Truman told Jackson the kind of man he desired as General Counsel. The specifications were precisely those Jackson himself was using in building up his own staff. Nevertheless, to help his good friend, Jackson parted with one of his good men.

He was Hugh Fulton and he would come to the committee fresh from the successful prosecution of Hopson, the utility magnate; Fox, the movie magnate; and other big-name executives who had run afoul the law. There was a slight period of waiting involved while Fulton polished off some of the odds and ends of pending litigation. Truman didn't care much for the delay, but suppressed his impatience.

"What do you think of him, Bill?" Truman asked eagerly

the day Fulton reported. Hardly less eager than Truman himself to meet Fulton, I had just ended a little chat with him in Truman's office. "He's got the stuff," Truman went on enthusiastically, answering his own question. "He knows what to do and I'm told he's a glutton for work. We're going places!"

"How much will he set you back?" I inquired.

"Nine thousand a year. He's worth more, but that's the limit we can pay him."

When Fulton started his work there was so much to investigate that he hardly knew where to begin.

Contractors and their agents had swarmed to Washington, and practically every get-rich-quick lawyer and layman in the capital had become a contract broker. The billions pouring from the Treasury to the hinterland offered dazzling opportunities for fees and commissions.

Business men who wanted to share in those billions soon found they had to come to Washington and get in the scramble. Or they had to send agents to represent them, and generally such representatives were unfamiliar with the ways of Washington. The alternative was to hire agents living in Washington who supposedly knew where to go and whom to see to get business.

The contractor who stayed home and hoped for government orders to come his way got none in those days; the man on the spot got the business.

Until the defense program roared into Washington, it had been a pleasant and comfortable city. Most residents of social or business standing knew members of Congress; relations between them and officialdom were pleasant. The incoming hordes of order-seekers, for the most part, knew

[163]

no members of Congress; when they were given a brush-off in their first contacts with officials, as they generally were, many of them concluded that it was necessary to pull wires and use "influence" to get contracts.

Most of Washington's brokers hadn't been brokers at all the week before. They multiplied like rabbits to serve the incoming suckers. And while some of them were willing to accept clients on a contingent-fee basis, they generally wanted a down payment by way of retainer.

The cocktail lounges of the city's crowded hotels buzzed with gossip of big contracts got through the influence of brokers. Often members of Congress were mentioned by name as allied with the brokers, and among some of the prospective contractors there was a fixed impression that the brokers divided their fees with official fixers.

Truman knew of this gossip. He was given names of senators, representatives, and other officials mentioned as fixers. He was given nothing more tangible. I asked him if the committee would investigate these tales.

"We are not going to be smear artists," he said. "If there's anything true in those stories it will come to light in our investigation. We have power to investigate all records."

Nevertheless, the committee took a side glance at the gossip. In his first annual report to the Senate, Truman said:

"[There is] the widespread belief, especially among small and intermediate business men, that Government officials can be 'reached,' which makes them credulous dupes of peddlers of 'influence' who approach them furtively with stories of their close connections at Washington, and promises of contracts if they are paid a commission, usually five or ten per cent of the contract price.

"In most instances the Washington connections are non-existent, and the peddlers of influence are simply acting on the chance that the business man in question can obtain a contract without help if he would make a serious and determined effort.

"In many instances, all the peddlers do is to disclose information as to contracts about to be negotiated which they have gleaned from Government sources available to all. The practice is difficult to expose and eliminate because the business men who are duped by it hate to admit that their avarice led them to attempt what they thought was bribery of Government procurement officers. In many cases where they obtain no contracts they have no way of proving the attempted extortion.

"The same situation exists with respect to those who actually do have the connections they boast of, the principal differences in their cases being that the Government is even more seriously injured and the offenders can more easily be subjected to criminal punishment.

"The committee has information with respect to a number of cases, some of which the committee will take up in future hearings. The committee has noted, however, that in most instances the businessmen so approached have not obtained sufficient evidence to establish the exact nature of the case. The committee believes that legislation to alleviate the evils inherent in lobbying should be studied."

The full story of official corruption incidental to the award of Government contracts still awaits disclosure. It is not a pretty story. It has come to light, in part, as this is written.

What Truman called "the appalling waste" of money in building new Army camps was the first thing his committee investigated.

"I am sorry to say that I do not think the Army has done a good job on camp construction," he told the Senate in August, a few months after the committee's investigators had taken to the field.

"There has been a lack of foresight and planning and a large amount of inefficiency, as a result of which I believe that several hundreds of millions of dollars have been wasted.

"As an Army officer I had always assumed that the War Department had paid some attention to the bitter lessons with respect to camp construction which we learned during the last war. I had assumed that when the time came, carefully drawn up plans would be taken from the files and put into operation with a minimum of delay.

"I was utterly astounded to find that although a postwar study had been made of camp construction problems encountered in the World War, all the copies thereof had been lost by the War Department; . . . that the generals in charge of planning for construction by the General Staff did not even conceive the possibility that we should ever again have a mobilization such as in 1917, involving the necessity of housing and training troops in barracks camps. . . .

"I found that the answer was not that Congress was niggardly with the Army . . . but that it was that the armchair generals in charge of such matters, although they knew that W.P.A. funds could be obtained for the purpose of planning projects, did not think it was worth while, or even possible, for the Army to use such funds to any advantage.

"If our plans for military campaigns are no more extensive and no better than those for construction, we are indeed in a deplorable situation."

There was more of this kind of strong denunciation and it was played up in the press. The Truman committee was making a good start, editors agreed. However painful such blunt statements may have been to Administration leaders, they caught the fancy of the man in the street.

No longer was Harry Truman merely another New Deal senator. IIe was talking about mismanagement in words that the public and the New Deal leaders alike could understand. And the Senate no longer had a choice as to giving him more money with which to continue his exposures; it would not have dared to deny it.

More money was voted by the Senate without a dissenting voice whenever Harry Truman asked for it. The grudging fifteen thousand dollars to start his committee on its way were followed by grants running as high as one hundred thousand dollars apiece.

When Truman told the Senate about the camp construction plans drawn up and lost, he was speaking of what he had found from personal inquiry. Brigadier General Charles D. Hartman was the officer who had drawn up the plans. As the Army's Constructing Quartermaster, General Hartman was in charge of clearing camp construction plans in 1941 when Truman addressed the Senate.

An honest, efficient but rather easy-going officer, General

Hartman had been through the First World War. Years later he had supervised the voluminous planning program to expand Army camps quickly should the need arise again.

He knew of the mistakes that had been made in the First World War and had undertaken to prevent their repetition. At one time there were eighty specialists working under his direction. By 1935 the draft of the expansion program was completed. It was typed, but not printed, and bound in five volumes which reportedly were placed in the library of the Army War College at Washington.

After finishing this work, General Hartman was sent elsewhere. When he returned to Washington in 1940 to take charge of the camp construction program for the national defense, he called for those volumes. They had disappeared. The results of his long labor and planning which had cost the Government several thousand dollars simply had vanished.

"We have paid a terrific price for lack of planning and inefficiency," Truman told the Senate, "but I hope and believe the War Department has learned some real lessons and that in the camp-construction program now being planned it will not make the same mistakes. I know it is already taking steps to remedy many of the defects to which my committee has drawn attention."

Big Business was still Harry Truman's pet peeve, however, and in his speech he took another fling at it.

"Our records will show," he said, "that more than three billion dollars in defense contracts have been let to just four companies.

"I am not opposed to that if it is absolutely necessary, but there is not any reason why those four companies could not make a distribution of the three billion dollars of contracts in such a way that the little people would not be put out of business by priorities and things of that kind which are now staring them in the face.

"No judgment at all has been used on the priority business."

Little businessmen pricked up their ears. By the thousands they deluged Congress with tales of their troubles. Some were facing bankruptcy, others were struggling to remain solvent in the hope that presently the great new customer in the market, Uncle Sam, would not pass them by.

Senators from many sections were receiving these letters. For the time, they forgot Party lines and united to compel the Government to award its contracts more widely. On one occasion, a bi-partisan group of seventeen senators went down to the War Department (Truman was not among them) to demand a more equitable share of this business for their constituents.

Suddenly Harry Truman had become a leading champion of Small Business. Big Business might hate him, but Small Business loved him then for those kind words he had spoken in its behalf. Well did even the dullards in the Senate know that while Big Business commanded relatively few votes on election day, Small Business voted in regiments and brigades.

Who were senators to deny further funds to a colleague hitting such a noble lick for Small Business? Let the question perish; they didn't.

Chapter Nine

===============✱===============

HARRY TRUMAN had merely glimpsed the sordid scene at Washington when he made his first address to the Senate as Chairman of its Defense Investigating Committee. He knew about the sweaty scramble for Government contracts, and something of the greed of Big Business and Big Labor. Of the law of the jungle behind the scenes he knew not a hundredth part.

Amazing details now crowded upon him. The little tyrannies of local labor unions were as peanuts. The shelving of Small Business plants that had distressed him was only a pawn's move in a great game for power and preference played in downtown Washington offices behind the curtain of the national defense.

He was to read the sorry story fast. It whirled in from almost every essential work of preparation for war; from steel, aluminum, copper, rayon, aircraft, food, rubber, manpower. The lid he lifted covered the seething activity of cross-purposes and conflicts in which self-defense came first and national defense second.

[170]

Over his forty-month chairmanship, Truman told the Senate in thirty reports what was going on behind the curtain. For his investigation the Senate voted, from time to time, a total of four hundred thousand dollars. It was a good investment for the country and it meant a liberal education in Government economy, its use and misuse, for Harry Truman. More intimately than any other person in the country, Truman knew in a few months what was going on behind the scenes and the motives behind such activity.

He had hardly assumed his role as investigator when the first emergency rapped at his door. On the step were John L. Lewis and a stoppage of work in the bituminous coal fields. The stoppage had brought the defense program to the brink of disaster.

As usual, Lewis was demanding a wage increase for the miners. Or, rather, wages increases; approximately seventeen per cent at northern mines and twenty-five per cent at southern mines. The miners' annual contract with the operators had expired and work had been halted. A bitter fight, of which the public knew little, was raging over the wage differential between northern and southern groups of coal operators.

Truman summoned Lewis and representatives of the operators before his committee. A forenoon session was held at which testimony developed that neither side had the slightest intention of yielding. There was no afternoon session. Instead, Truman and his colleagues sent word to southern operators substantially as follows:

"Your faction is holding up the settlement. We know your mines are owned by northern capitalists and bankers. If you don't end this deadlock within twenty-four hours, we are going to send for these capitalists and bankers. We intend to put them on the witness stand and find out from them, as principals, whether the national safety or the wage dispute comes first."

That night the deadlock was broken. The miners went back to work at once.

It was Truman's first effective blow for the defense program. Others were to follow. One of the first was a bold move to terminate the dual Capital-Labor control set up by Roosevelt to direct defense production.

Subordinate to the President alone, the dominant agency was the Office of Production Management. The late Sidney Hillman and William S. Knudsen were co-directors. Hillman was a Left-wing labor leader; Knudsen, an industrialist and former high official of General Motors Corporation. Hillman was given authority by Roosevelt to run the labor end of the production program; Knudsen, the industrial end.

Nobody sat in the driver's seat. The reins were in two pairs of hands. Dollar-a-year and W.O.C. workers who had come to Washington by the hundreds took their orders from the dual control.

Harry Truman had the good sense to realize at once that such a division of authority could wreck the defense program. Many an industrialist and many another member of Congress thought so, too. While they criticized the set-up and did nothing to change it, Truman acted. In the name of his committee, he demanded that the division of authority end.

In so doing, he crossed swords with Sidney Hillman.

It is doubtful if Truman knew at that time of the strong ties between Roosevelt and Hillman, or how far back they went, or how they originated. Those details were not known then or later to the general public, but the bond was real and substantial, dating back to 1937 and the break between Roosevelt and John L. Lewis.

There had been a hot fight that year at the annual convention of the C.I.O. over the election of its secretary. Harry Bridges, maritime labor leader of the West Coast, wanted the place and came near winning it despite the opposition of the Lewis forces. Lewis then was President of the C.I.O.

A year earlier, Lewis had made $500,000 available to the Democratic high command to help re-elect Roosevelt. Why that was done, aside from the undeniable fact that Roosevelt was Labor's outstanding champion, was the subject of considerable speculation. In some quarters there was a strong impression that Lewis wanted to get rid of Miss Frances Perkins as Secretary of Labor; and that he felt such substantial financial support would influence Roosevelt to replace her.

If so, he was mistaken. Miss Perkins remained in the Cabinet, and Lewis broke with the President.

There was also a conviction in certain Labor quarters that Miss Perkins had played a hidden part in the fight to have Harry Bridges elected Secretary of the C.I.O. It was a fight Hillman supported. Had Bridges won in the contest with Lewis, he would have been in position later to attempt Lewis' overthrow as C.I.O. head.

After Bridges lost, Hillman became the rallying point within the C.I.O. of the anti-Lewis forces. Miss Perkins presented Hillman to the President. Roosevelt received him graciously, liked him from the start, and saw him thereafter with fair frequency. Hillman then was nurturing the anti-Lewis elements in C.I.O., a move Roosevelt undoubtedly would have approved had he known of it —and he may have known of it.

As the organization's annual convention neared, in November, 1940, Hillman was convinced that he had the votes to defeat Lewis for re-election as C.I.O. President.

In the last days of the 1940 Presidential campaign, Lewis delivered an anti-Roosevelt radio address in which he announced he would step down from the C.I.O. presidency if Roosevelt were re-elected. Hillman and his supporters regarded that speech as melodramatics; they were confident they could defeat Lewis, anyhow, and they thought Lewis knew of their ability to do so.

Such was the background of Roosevelt's strong liking for Sidney Hillman, the labor leader seeking to oust John L. Lewis, one of Roosevelt's bitterest critics, from power.

If Harry Truman knew that, it made no difference. He was determined that Hillman would have to go as co-director of O.P.M., along with Knudsen. Authority over the program would have to be vested in one man, Truman felt, if defense production were to be effective.

In an address to the Senate on October 29, 1941, Truman hotly condemned Hillman.

The immediate cause of Truman's wrath was a reported attempt by Hillman (which Hillman denied) to have a construction contract withheld from the low bidder, the Currier Company. The American Federation of Labor dominated the building trades unions and Hillman reportedly feared that an award to the Currier firm would be followed by labor troubles.

"A responsible company has made a low bid," Truman told the Senate, "which it is prepared to perform and is capable of performing if not illegally interfered with. Mr. Sidney Hillman advises that it be denied the contract and that the taxpayers pay several hundred thousand dollars more because Mr. Hillman fears trouble from what he calls irresponsible elements of the American Federation of Labor.

"I cannot condemn Mr. Hillman's position too strongly. First, the United States does not fear trouble from any source; and if trouble is threatened, the United States is able to protect itself. If Mr. Hillman cannot or will not protect the interests of the United States, I am in favor of replacing him with someone who can and will. . . .

"The Department of Justice has already ruled that it would be illegal . . . to disregard the low bid. I am going to ask the Attorney General to keep closely informed as to developments in this matter, and I know he will perform his duty and see to it that anyone violating the laws of the United States will be apprehended and tried."

Truman was speaking of Sidney Hillman, chief figure in Roosevelt's instructions to "clear everything with Sidney" at the Democratic nominating convention at Chicago three years later.

These were harsh words to level at Roosevelt's Labor protégé at the very top of the defense program. A few years earlier, Truman in similar circumstances might have held his tongue. But not now; the words came now from the lips of a Truman self-dedicated to serve his country to the best of his ability in his official position.

And they were hard for him to utter because they easily could be construed as anti-Labor. Truman was the antithesis of anti-Labor. He was altogether pro-Labor, although he was disgusted then, as later, with the grasping antics of some of Labor's high priests.

But first of all, Harry Truman was pro-America.

There was no doubting the courage of Truman's act. How high Hillman stood at the White House had been summarized, with considerable bombast, three years earlier by Hillman's friends. The summary was contained in a pamphlet entitled "Brain Trust" issued by the American Labor Party in September, 1938. An excerpt read as follows:

"Next to John L. Lewis, Sidney Hillman is the most powerful leader in the C.I.O. Next to Corcoran and Cohen, Franklin D. Roosevelt likes Sidney best. Next to Browder, Hillman is closest to Moscow."

Truman's first glance at O.P.M. in the early days of his investigation disclosed that Hillman and Knudsen held virtually unlimited power over the billions the government was spending. By order of Roosevelt, all defense contracts involving the payment of $500,000 or more were "cleared" through this dual control.

That included the construction program of the Army for its new camps, munition plants, and flying fields; for its tens of thousands of supply items from gasoline to shoes; for its armaments of every sort, such as tanks, planes, ordnance, and rifles. It was equally binding on the

Navy. It covered work on naval and air bases acquired from Britain. It blanketed defense housing. In a word, it applied to everything bought in the name of national defense not omitting purchases to be made later under the Lend-Lease program.

Over that stupendous volume of spending, Sidney Hillman—described by his friends as "next to Browder, closest to Moscow"—held, with William S. Knudsen, the determining voice. Army, Navy, and other agencies were authorized to proceed with preliminary negotiations involving $500,000 or more of public funds, but they were forbidden to execute contracts without first obtaining approval of the Hillman-Knudsen over-all agency.

Truman looked further.

He found that as a consequence, Knudsen and Hillman quite properly had advance information as to every proposed purchase of supplies or services amounting to $500,-000 or more. They knew at all times what was to be bought, in what volume, at what cost and from what firms. And Hillman, of course, knew what plants were marked for contracts; whether those plants were friendly or unfriendly to Organized Labor; whether their forces were union or non-union.

The advance knowledge of this mountainous volume of business, *and its labor relations,* was known, of course, to the score or more top-flight labor leaders with which Hillman surrounded himself at O.P.M. He and his satellites were in position to unionize all industry.

And Truman found that Hillman had worked with great speed and effectiveness to exercise his vast powers.

Hillman had started his work in the defense program as

a member of the Advisory Commission to the National Defense in the autumn of 1940, a time when Truman was fighting for re-election. The ill-starred Commission was predecessor to O.P.M. One of Hillman's early acts as a member of the Commission was to bring before that body the status of firms, such as the Ford Motor Company, which had defied the National Labor Relations Board.

In some of those outstanding cases, including the Ford Company, the courts had not passed finally on the Board's rulings that the Wagner Act (National Labor Relations law) had been violated. Hillman maintained that a final court decision was unnecessary; that a finding of violation by only the Board was sufficient to bar any firm from obtaining a negotiated contract with the Government under the national defense program.

Hillman swung the Advisory Commission, which he dominated almost from its inception, to his viewpoint. He then went to the White House and Roosevelt approved the Commission's finding. Hillman then saw to it, with characteristic energy and speed, that no time was lost in passing the word to the Army, Navy, and other defense agencies, warning them to negotiate no contracts with firms which the Labor Relations Board held to have been in violation of the Wagner Act.

Compliance by those agencies was immediate.

To drive the last legal rivet home, Hillman made oral request of Robert H. Jackson, then Attorney General, for a formal ruling. On October 2, 1940, Jackson obliged informally. He wrote Hillman as follows:

"We have given informal consideration to your oral request for advice as to the effect of findings by the National

Labor Relations Board that an employer is in violation of the National Labor Relations Act.

"It seems too clear to admit of controversy, though we will prepare a formal opinion if it is requested through the usual channels, that the findings of the National Labor Relations Board that an employer is in violation of the National Labor Relations Act are binding and conclusive upon the other agencies of the executive branch of the Government unless and until these findings are reversed by a court of competent jurisdiction."

Whether Hillman used this ruling to block a multi-million dollar contract to Ford Motor Company for airplane engines was the subject of speculation soon after Jackson made his informal ruling. Some development behind O.P.M.'s closed doors did operate to call off the deal.

At that time, the Ford Company was beating off energetically C.I.O.'s vigorous efforts to unionize its plant. A huge contract for the Ford Company was in the making, but it did not materialize; and there were mile-wide discrepancies concerning it in the statements issued at Washington and Dearborn.

It was reported currently in Washington that the War Department had actually signed the contract (that was before the President ordered all big contracts cleared through O.P.M.), that members of the Advisory Commission other than Hillman had signed it, and that Hillman would have no truck with it. Edsel Ford made a quick trip to Washington to view the snarl. Whatever the details, the contract was not executed.

C.I.O.'s rival, the American Federation of Labor, was quick to benefit from Hillman's master stroke. Army camp construction was the first big spending program to get under way, and most of the workers in the building trades were A.F.L. members.

Truman estimated that approximately 490,000 men were employed on the far-flung camp construction program at its peak. Hillman had opened the door to unionization of the entire force. With scant preparation, Labor embarked in the wholesale business of recruiting.

Contractors at all camps had been notified of the Army's labor policy which was in line with the Jackson ruling sent informally to Hillman. They wanted to avoid trouble and the easy way out was to refer all applicants for jobs to union organizers. At most, but not all, of the camps that course was followed. Men who could not show union cards simply were not hired; if they didn't have cards, they were told to get them.

At Fort Meade, Maryland, where a mammoth construction job was snapped through at high speed, Truman's investigation revealed that nobody was hired unless okayed by the unions. That applied to common laborers as well as skilled mechanics.

The unions there charged carpenters $57.50 apiece for work permits; common laborers, $25 apiece. Some of the needy applicants came almost penniless for the work, and these were permitted by the union to pay for their work permits by installments. Truman estimated that approximately $200,000 was taken in by the unions for work permits at that one construction job.

At other camps it was much the same. Fees had a wide spread. One union set $300 as its price for a work permit. All such charges were a union tax on a non-union man's right to work, and the general rule was, "No work permit, no job."

Camp construction was well under way when Truman started his investigation. Many thousands of workers already had paid for their work permits. It was too late for him to move for the return of fees to those who had paid them, but not too late to end the impost on workers yet to be employed. Truman moved at once to end it.

"Cut it out," was the word he sent the labor leaders concerned. He warned them as a friend of Labor. In most cases, although not all, the warning was heeded. To the Senate, Truman said:

"The committee is investigating the general question of union fees in defense industries and expects to determine to what extent this practice became a mere racket."

Labor's irregularities lay largely on the surface of events where all could see them. They were dwarfed by Industry's operations hidden behind the curtain of the defense program. Truman discovered that at the outset of his investigation. The program had been in operation nearly ten months when his committee started to function, and billions of dollars in contracts had been parceled out when he started asking questions.

It was too late to unscramble those eggs but not too late to look closely at them. Truman looked.

The tight little group of machine-tool manufacturers, he learned, had been among the first to benefit. Composed of about two hundred fifty companies and dominated by a score of the largest, its representatives took luxurious quarters at Washington's swank Carlton Hotel in June, 1940.

They guarded their affairs closely. No outsider could serve even as secretary of their trade association; the post long had been filled by one of their own trusted company's officials.

Only the larger companies were represented. Behind closed doors they met to do business with officers of the Army and the Navy. Before them those officers spread, like many gems tossed on a table top, the vast prospective machinery needs of a doubled Navy and an Army of two million men.

In the days of negotiation that followed, the machine-tool business necessary to meet those needs was divided among the score or so of dominant companies. An occasional crumb was dropped from the table for their own little ones.

When the group left Washington at the close of negotiations they carried home many million dollars in contracts. The windfall mortgaged their production far ahead; one big firm reportedly was assured of Government orders to keep it busy for five years—at a time when the defense program was calling for all possible speed.

Months later, when the big companies were working overtime and the little companies were crying for work, the Government tried to crack down. It insisted that the big fellows disgorge to subcontractors some of the business they themselves couldn't get around to for months. At a closed meeting Knudsen read the riot act, or its trade equivalent. They were hot with anger; and when an inkling reached the press, they released a statement for publication. For a resentful group, it was a tame and judicious statement.

Knudsen's stinging rap on their knuckles knocked some of the Government's orders from their hands and into smaller plants.

At approximately the time of the Carlton meetings, the rush of business men to Washington started. In a few weeks it resembled a stampede. They did not stay at home waiting for invitations to help the country. On the contrary, they came by fast train and airplane, unbidden except for a comparative few, to press claims for recognition, eager to join the promising new set-up, pulling wires to get on.

Some of them went to work for a dollar a year. Many more went to work without compensation. The latter were the W.O.C.'s; Truman had a listing made of them. It contained hundreds of names.

The dollar-a-year men and the W.O.C.'s, Truman's listing disclosed, had fared well. Between June 1, 1940, and April 30, 1941, the Army and Navy had given contracts totaling $2,880,450,000 to sixty-six firms whose officials or former officials had served the Government at a dollar a year or without compensation during that period.

These huge orders extending over the eleven-month period at the start of the defense program were by no means the full total. The listing covered only the larger firms. How much the smaller fry got wasn't listed.

Time and again, Truman found, there had been fierce under-cover fighting among business firms for a division of the spoils. An outstanding case concerned the Army jeep.

In 1938 the American Bantam Car Company, a million-dollar corporation with a plant at Butler, Pennsylvania, conceived the idea of the jeep. The Army, upon inquiry, said it was interested. Over a period of nearly two years the company perfected the vehicle at its own expense. The Army's interest increased correspondingly.

In February, 1940, the company's president, Francis H. Fenn, employed Charles A. Payne to represent the company in its dealings with the Army at Washington.

The Army ordered 70 pilot models of the jeep on July 25, 1940, at a price of approximately $2,500 apiece. The models withstood the stiff tests of the Army, and four months later the company was given an order for 1,500 jeeps at a price of about $1,000 a car, or $1,519,000 for the lot.

The dollar marks on the contract automatically brought it before O.P.M. through the "clearance" ordered on all contracts of $500,000 or more.

In the meantime, Payne had written Knudsen, co-director of O.P.M., offering the Government "the complete facilities of our plant for production" of the new vehicle. The letter, or word of its contents, was passed along to O.P.M.'s Chief of Production, John D. Biggers of Toledo, Ohio, who had left his business to help the Government at Washington. Fenn called on Biggers.

"He told me at that time," Fenn testified under oath before Truman, "that he had nothing against the Bantam Car Company. But he said we were a small company and he doubted our ability to produce the cars in the quantity needed.

"We set up our plant for production. Our entire assembly line was torn up and rearranged. Parts of the machine shop were torn down and the rest rearranged. We tooled up for production.

"The Reconstruction Finance Corporation made us a loan and our assembly line became a jeep-car assembly line. Soon we were turning out 65 cars a day. We were tooled up so we could turn out from 275 to 300 jeeps a day by running three shifts."

At about that time, Fenn continued, a high Army officer became convinced that the company shouldn't be given too much of that business. Fenn identified the officer as Major General R. C. Moore, Deputy Chief of Staff to General George C. Marshall. General Moore, Fenn said, apparently felt that other automobile makers were larger and financially stronger; that they doubtless were better able to go into quantity production.

Another order for 1,500 jeeps was placed. That went to the Ford Motor Company. A third order of the same size was given to the Willys-Overland Company at Toledo. The Ford Company apparently knew little of the jeep.

"I personally saw Ford Motor Company representatives under our car at a grease pit at Holabird (Baltimore Depot) making free-hand drawings of the lay-out," Fenn testified under oath.

In April, 1941, the Bantam plant was visited, Fenn continued, by two men; one an officer of Army's G-4; the other from the office of the Assistant Secretary of War. Not long thereafter the company, then nearing completion of its 1,500-car order, was given a contract for 1,000 more jeeps. And that was all.

"We had to slow down production," Fenn told the Truman committee. "In order to keep our key men together we had to go on a schedule of 15 cars a day instead of 65."

That was at a time when various branches of the Army, the committee learned from War Department correspondence, were clamoring for more jeeps. The vehicle had found favor and it was apparent that a big production order would be given soon. Bantam Company officials estimated it at about 16,000 cars—sufficient to keep the company busy ten months at the 65-cars-a-day schedule, or little more than four months at three-shift capacity.

Specifications covering the jeep were rewritten in the War Department without consulting the Bantam Company. Manufacturers were invited to submit bids, among them the Bantam Company.

"We received the specifications on Monday," Fenn told Truman, "and the bids were to be opened the following Tuesday."

The order was to be for 16,000 cars, "all or none." That meant the successful bidder would get the full amount and the other bidders would get nothing.

The Bantam Company, after hectic work, submitted its bid on time. Its offer was $40 a car higher than the low bid. The order went to the Willys-Overland Company; the Bantam Company lost the big contract on its own device. Willys-Overland Company, which had been bankrupt, at once was given a $3,000,000 loan by the Reconstruction Finance Corporation.

Diversion of the big order was forerunner to a stupendous development affecting the entire automobile industry.

"We have no business to produce cars not essential to defense," Truman told me one day in the summer of 1941. "We need steel, iron, copper, glass, manpower for the national defense. We are now using large tonnages for building pleasure cars.

"The automobile industry ought to be converted to the production of planes, tanks, munitions and other defense matériel. It would be a good thing if the Government shut down every automobile plant in the United States and had them converted as quickly as possible to essential production.

"We would need a small number of passenger cars and probably a larger number of trucks for replacements. Arrangements could be made to produce limited numbers for the defense program; the other automobile plants should go in for essential production."

There was strong opposition within the industry to any such radical change. Truman discussed the idea with his fellow committeemen and with downtown officials. In the latter part of 1941 the Truman group unanimously urged its adoption.

The strong recommendation weakened the downtown opposition.

An outstanding dollar-a-year man who spearheaded the opposition could not be convinced, however, that reconversion was desirable. A strange thing happened: One day, unexpectedly, it was announced that this man had been sent to London. Quickly thereafter the Truman view prevailed.

For the first time in the history of the automobile industry assembly lines throughout the country were idle. They were dismantled. Automobile production ceased and the huge plants were tooled for defense production. Not only auto plants; others producing certain civilian goods likewise were reconverted.

It was during those stirring days that Truman's demand for ending dual control at O.P.M. bore fruit.

"The result," Truman modestly told the Senate later, "was the appointment of Donald Nelson and the creation of the War Production Board."

Defense troubles came in clusters to Truman and his committeemen. There was, for instance, a vast prospective shortage of aluminum for building bombers. Truman unearthed the facts with speed and energy. His revelations were followed by large grants of Government funds for building mammoth new aluminum plants and the output of this metal was stepped up to meet war needs.

For another thing, Truman and his associates were quick to realize the vital importance of strong airpower. They nagged the War Production Board for months until it set up a section charged with over-all planning for aircraft production and placed a notable industrialist, Charles E. Wilson, at its head.

Again, the Truman group—as if it had nothing else to do—revealed the unpleasant facts concerning the nation's dwindling supply of natural rubber. Truman reported to the Senate:

"At the very period when it became clear that some action was necessary to conserve rubber, the [civilian production] companies indulged in an orgy of consumption, laying in stocks of finished goods at a rate which reached in June, 1941, a new high of over a million tons a year."

With the aid of Jesse Jones, head of the Reconstruction Finance Corporation, the rubber program finally was adjusted, but not until Mr. Jones had been sharply criticized.

"The Committee believes," Truman told the Senate, "that Mr. Jones handled this situation expeditiously and ably. Although the relaxation of quota restrictions was not obtained soon enough to ease the situation, this was not attributable to any lack of energetic action on the part of Mr. Jones."

These were a few of the dozens of irons Harry Truman had in the fire of his investigation at the same time. He was by no means the whole committee. But he sparked the effort in fields of work essential to the defense program. The actual spadework was done generally by his committee's capable investigators and its hard-working General Counsel. Members of the committee joined Truman in putting aside political considerations in this period. They worked as one.

Conducting the investigation was a colossal job, but it did not keep Truman from the Senate floor. He was learning with blitz speed now, rising in senatorial stature, speaking no longer "off the cuff" but by the book, and citing verse and chapter. In those tumultuous days he was absorbing know-how as a dry sponge soaks up water. And in the Chamber he soon was regarded as the Senate's outstanding authority on all phases of the national defense. When he spoke his colleagues listened with a new respect.

"You look tired," I told him one day.

"I am, Bill," he replied. "I'm tired as a dog and having the time of my life."

Harry Truman's big job was to iron out the wrinkles in

[189]

the far-flung war production effort. It was job enough and he lived with it. Foreign relations, the delicate international situation, simply were not his dish at the time. He was intensely interested in the creeping approach of the war thunderhead in the diplomatic sky, but what to do about it he left to what he called "the proper authorities."

Downtown, however, a great many officials were volunteering ideas to Roosevelt and the State Department. These related mainly to formulas for preventing America's entry into the war.

Among those so engaged, in addition to his official duties, was Henry Morgenthau, Jr., Secretary of the Treasury. Morgenthau had a plan he thought was tops. He put it before the President and the State Department.

Germ of the Morgenthau plan was that the United States should spend five billion dollars plus to end the war in the Far East.

His memorandum to Roosevelt and Hull was dated November 19, 1941, less than three weeks before Pearl Harbor. At the State Department it was referred to Maxwell M. Hamilton, head of the Far Eastern (FE) Division. Maxwell reported to Hull that the "proposal is the most constructive one I have yet seen."

Japan at that time was at war with China only and was bound by treaty to Germany. Morgenthau's proposal roughly was that the United States, from its Treasury, lend Japan and China two billion dollars apiece; set up stabilization funds for currency of the two nations with another billion dollars of American taxpayers' funds; and lend money to China to buy Hong Kong back from the British.

The idea seems to have entranced the loyal Morgenthau who wrote ("Dear Cordell") Hull as follows:

"If the President were to propose something like the appended agreement and the Japanese accept, the whole world would be electrified by the successful transformation of a threatening and belligerent powerful enemy into a peaceful and prosperous neighbor.

"The prestige and leadership of the President both at home and abroad would skyrocket by so brilliant and momentous a diplomatic victory—a victory that required no vanquished, a victory that would immediately bring peace, happiness and prosperity to hundreds of millions of Eastern peoples and assure the subsequent defeat of Germany!"

Maxwell's letter to Hull and Morgenthau's "Strictly Confidential" outline of the proposal follow:

DEPARTMENT OF STATE
DIVISION OF FAR EASTERN AFFAIRS

November 19, 1941

STRICTLY CONFIDENTIAL

Mr. Secretary:

There is attached a revision of the proposal which was sent to you by Mr. Morgenthau. (The proposal still of course needs further revision and elaboration.)

I think that the proposal is the most constructive one which I have yet seen. I have shown the proposal to all of the senior officers of FE, and all of them concur in that view.

I urge that the most careful consideration be given

promptly to the proposal. To that end I suggest that copies of the proposal be made available to Admiral Stark and General Marshall and that you arrange to confer with them in regard to the matter as soon as they have had an opportunity to examine the proposal.

MMH

Tentative,
Without Comment

STRICTLY CONFIDENTIAL

OUTLINE OF PROPOSED BASIS
FOR AGREEMENT BETWEEN THE
UNITED STATES AND JAPAN

On its part the Government of the United States proposes to take the following steps:

1. To reduce to a normal footing American naval forces now in the Pacific waters, without of course, limiting in any way the freedom of action and of decision of the Government of the United States with regard to the disposition of naval forces in the United States.

2. To negotiate a multilateral non-aggression pact with Japan, China, the British Empire, The Netherlands, Thailand and Soviet Russia.

3. To suggest to the Chinese Government and to the Japanese Government that those Governments enter into peaceful negotiations with regard to the future status of Manchuria.

4. To enter into negotiations with the British, Chi-

nese, Dutch, Thai and Japanese Governments for the conclusion of an agreement whereunder each of the Governments would pledge itself to respect the territorial integrity of French Indochina and, in the event that there should develop a threat to the territorial integrity of Indochina, to enter into immediate consultation with a view to taking such measures as may be deemed necessary and advisable to meet the threat in question. Such agreements would provide also that each of the Governments party to the agreement would not seek or accept preferential treatment in its trade relations with Indochina and would use its influence to obtain for each of the signatories most-favored-nation treatment in trade and commerce with French Indochina.

5. To give up all extra-territorial rights in China, including rights and interests in and with regard to the International Settlements at Shanghai and Amoy, and rights under the Boxer Protocol of 1901.

To endeavor to obtain the agreement of the British Government to give up British extra-territorial rights in China, including rights in the international settlements and concessions and under the Boxer Protocol of 1901.

To use its influence toward causing the British Government to cede Hong Kong to China. (This provision might take the form of an understanding to use our influence with the British Government to cause the British Government to sell Hong Kong to China, the purchase price to be loaned to China by the United States.)

6. To recommend to Congress enactment of legislation to amend the Immigration Act of 1924 so as to place all peoples of all races on a quota basis.

7. To negotiate a trade agreement with Japan giving Japan (a) most-favored-nation treatment and (b) such concessions on Japanese imports into the United States as can be mutually satisfactorily arranged, including an agreement to bind raw silk on the free list.

To enter into a joint declaration between the United States and Japan with regard to commercial policy along the lines of the draft handed the Japanese Ambassador on November 15.

8. To extend to Japan a $2,000,000,000 20-year credit at two per cent interest, to be drawn upon at a rate not to exceed $200,000,000 a year except with the approval of the President of the United States.

(Note: The United States should be prepared to extend a similar credit to China.)

(Note: This provision presumably would require Congressional approval.)

9. To set up a $500,000,000 stabilization fund half supplied by Japan and half by the United States, to be used for the stabilization of the dollar-yen rate.

(Note: The United States should be prepared to act similarly in regard to China.)

(Note: This provision may require congressional approval.)

10. To remove the freezing restrictions on Japanese funds in the United States.

(B)

On its part the Government of Japan proposes to take the following steps:

1. To withdraw all military, naval, air and police forces from China (excluding Manchuria—see separate provisions) and from Indochina.

2. To withdraw all support—military, political, economic—from any Government or regime in China other than the Government of the National Republic of China with capital temporarily at Chungking.

3. To replace with yen currency at a rate to be agreed upon among the Treasuries of China, Japan, Great Britain and the United States, all Japanese Military scrip, yen and local regime notes circulating in China.

4. To give up all extra-territorial rights in China including rights in international settlements and concessions and rights under the Boxer Protocol.

5. To withdraw all Japanese troops from Manchuria except for a few divisions necessary as a police force, provided U.S.S.R. withdraws all her troops from the Far Eastern front except for an equivalent remainder.

6. To sell to the United States ——— tons of Japanese merchant shipping, to be delivered to the United States within three months of the signing of the present agreement; also to sell to the United States up to 50 per cent of Japan's current output of shipping, including naval and commercial ships, on a cost-plus-20-per cent basis as the United States may select, it

being understood that the United States will sell Japan such raw materials as it may be necessary for Japan to import for these purposes.

7. To negotiate a multilateral non-aggression pact with the United States, China, the British Empire, The Netherlands, Thailand and Soviet Russia.

8. To remove the freezing restrictions on American funds in Japan.

Such was Morgenthau's formula for ending the war in the Far East. It got nowhere at the White House. And Harry Truman kept on with his job of speeding war production.

Chapter Ten

———————✳———————

HARRY TRUMAN'S investigation of the defense program was highly important, but there were other things of even greater importance before Congress in 1941. Chief was legislation under which the United States was readying for war. In this were laws to authorize, among other things, much of the production program that Truman's committee investigated.

They were crowding fast upon Congress when Truman started his second senatorial term.

The Lend-Lease program was one. Truman supported this, and after it became law (March 11, 1941) voted in favor of a seven-billion-dollar appropriation to make it effective. In a subsequent report to the Senate Truman defined his understanding of Lend-Lease as follows, in part:

"We should never forget that Lend-Lease was originally authorized by Congress solely because the English and others whom we desired to assist did not have sufficient American exchange to purchase the materials needed by

[197]

them. Lend-Lease was never intended as a device to shift a portion of their war costs to us.

"Before authorizing Lend-Lease, Congress expressly requested and received assurances that Lend-Lease assistance would be extended only where the recipient was fully utilizing all of its own resources. Such resources, of course, include foreign-held American securities. . . ."

Lend-Lease was Roosevelt's idea. In the autumn of 1940 he discussed it enthusiastically with the Cabinet. Finally he asked his advisers to have their legal staffs prepare a proposed law to cover the program. Among the top legal brains at Washington keen rivalry developed to write the draft that would be acceptable to the President.

Roosevelt personally pored over the various drafts submitted and decided that the one prepared at the Treasury suited him best. It had been written by the Department's General Counsel, a young man from Syracuse, N. Y., named Edward H. Foley, Jr. Foley thus became the unpublicized author of the Lend-Lease Bill which was enacted with little change by Congress.

There was intense, but not numerically strong, opposition by isolationists in Congress to the Lend-Lease proposal.

Among their arguments was the claim that Great Britain had huge resources including big investments in the United States. Why, then, should Americans tax themselves to put weapons in her hands? This argument made an impression on public opinion. At that stage Morgenthau had a heart-to-heart talk with Lord Halifax, the British Ambassador. An outstanding gesture by Britain

[198]

would be helpful, Morgenthau suggested, in overcoming congressional opposition to the Lend-Lease Bill.

Halifax was agreeable and apparently started the preliminaries. Four days after the Lend-Lease Bill became law a deal was made in New York between a group of American bankers and officials of the British Government. It was the aftermath of Morgenthau's suggestion that the British give a token of their Lend-Lease appreciation by selling one of their American investments.

Under its terms, the British parted with the largest rayon company in the world, the American Viscose Corporation. Its seven plants covered more than 8,000,000 square feet of floor space and were spread over 1,430 acres at locations in three states. Original cost to the British owners had been $133,839,286, but somewhat more than half of that had been written off gradually on the books. Value of the plants in March, 1941, was carried at $66,467,758.

In addition, the corporation had in its vaults cash, stocks, bonds and other so-called quick assets which were worth $55,070,195 on the depressed market. Total assets were carried on the books at $121,537,963.

The American bankers paid the British Government $54,348,286—in two payments—for everything.

That was less than the market value of the quick assets alone.

Ten weeks later a syndicate of seventeen American brokers recapitalized the corporation, named it the American Viscose Company, and sold its stock to the public for $62,193,600. Gross profit to the syndicate amounted to more than $7,800,000. Out of that sum, however, were paid underwriting, management, and other pertinent expenses.

It was reported in Washington that the British corporation was owned largely by English noblemen and that the Royal Family had shareholders' interests in it. Another report also reached the Truman committee: That the United States Government, through the Reconstruction Finance Corporation, had been willing to *lend* the British owners $75,000,000 with the properties as collateral and permit them to retain their ownership of the corporation.

Apparently this word reached the British too late. They went through with the deal. They stood by the sorry bargain and sold their holdings outright for $20,000,000 less than they reportedly could have borrowed on them.

That was reverse Lend-Lease not contemplated under the new law. Morgenthau thought the deal altogether too shrewd. Although no public announcement was made, it was reported that he succeeded in having the American bankers increase their payment to the British by approximately $1,000,000.

The Viscose Company deal was beyond the Truman committee's pale and was not investigated by that group. Details of a somewhat related transaction, however, were placed before Truman and his associates. This involved a loan in American cash—Lend-Lease did not cover cash loans—of $425,000,000 by the Reconstruction Finance Corporation to the British Government in the summer of 1941.

Jesse Jones, R.F.C. head, handled the details.

Mr. Jones wanted plenty of collateral and the British put it in his hands. Some of it consisted of millions of shares of stock in American corporations. Listed common stocks of outstanding American companies included in the collateral were as follows, in part:

American Rolling Mill, 133,000 shares.
American Telephone & Telegraph, 70,000 shares.
American Tobacco B, 34,000 shares.
Chrysler Corporation, 36,000 shares.
Commercial Investment Trust, 59,000 shares.
Eastman Kodak, 57,000 shares.
First National Bank of New York, 103,000 shares.
General Motors Corporation, 434,000 shares.
Great Northern Railway, 44,000 shares (preferred).
National Biscuit Company, 60,000 shares.
Public Service Corp. of New Jersey, 24,000 shares.
Sears Roebuck & Company, 47,000 shares.
Socony-Vacuum Oil Company, 130,000 shares.
Standard Oil Company of New Jersey, 180,000 shares.
U. S. Steel Corporation 21,000 shares (preferred).
Westinghouse Air Brake Company, 40,000 shares.
Woolworth Company, 247,000 shares.

The foregoing and other securities had been assembled by the British Treasury under Orders in Council requiring British investors to turn over such holdings to the Government. There also were many millions of dollars' worth of bonds and debentures of American corporations. And there was an impressively long list of unlisted securities

[201]

estimated to be worth (at market prices then prevailing) about $115,000,000. The value of the listed securities in the collateral was approximately $205,000,000.

Nor was that all. Another item in the collateral was described by Mr. Jones as follows:

"Capital stock of 41 British-owned United States insurance companies estimated to have an aggregate net worth of something over $180,000,000. The going-concern value of the insurance companies is substantially more than this figure."

Listed by name, as they were, the companies form an impressive list doing a huge annual business in the United States. However, there was still more collateral, namely:

"In addition, earnings of the United States branches of 41 British insurance companies not incorporated in this country. The net assets of these branches in this country . . . is approximately $200,000,000, consisting largely of cash and United States Government securities."

Apparently the entire insurance business of Great Britain in the United States was included in the collateral.

Interest and dividends on the collateral, plus the earnings of the insurance companies, approximated $36,-000,000 annually over the preceding five years. All of it, Mr. Jones said, "will be applied to the payment of the interest and principal of the loan."

R.F.C. charged the British three per cent on the loan, approximately half as much again as the United States Government had to pay on the funds which were borrowed from the American public. With the collateral yielding much more than three per cent, Mr. Jones estimated that the debt would be wiped out at the end of fifteen years.

The United States Government stands to make a tidy profit on this loan during the fifteen-year period. The British got the money when they could get it nowhere else. And the United States got ample security and a profit along with it.

The lurking fears of the Senate oligarchy in setting up the Truman committee soon proved unjustified. The insurance policy against his Party irregularity was unnecessary. Harry Truman needed no guard of hundred-per cent New Dealers on his committee to keep him in line with the Roosevelt policies. Far from it; he saw the world more and more through Liberal eyes; his maturer judgment guided him even further to the Left.

His senatorial buddies, to the last mother's son, were of the Left-wing group. Some of them were very, very Liberal. Some presided over little nests of radical workers stuck away in the spacious rooms of the Senate Office Building. They were the working staffs that produced the ideas which were written into numerous bills bedeviling the Conservatives. Dozens of these radical workers and their downtown kith and kin were carded in the files of the House Committee on Un-American Activities among thousands allied with Communist-front, fellow-traveler, and political-action groups.

Personnel of these radical staffs at the Capitol came largely as loans from the downtown agencies. It was the vogue of certain senatorial groups to indulge in such borrowing. The arrangement was agreeable and convenient, for committee funds were limited and the borrowed work-. ers were paid by the agencies from which they were borrowed. The tight-fisted policy of the Senate purse-strings committee cramped. the style of Leftist members with mile-high notions. It limited their scope in planning fresh and daring laws regarded as cock-eyed by the Conservatives. Borrowed personnel was the answer.

Money thus spent in efforts to make the postwar world more to the Leftists' liking came from the common jackpot filled by the nation's taxpayers. The War Production Board, the Federal Housing Administration, the Office of Price Administration were frequent lenders of personnel. They sent their advanced thinkers drawing salaries up to $9,000 a year to spark advanced-thinking members of Congress, but they carried those salaries in their annual budgets. Thus the funds going to such agencies not only were spent for planning war production, for Federal housing, for price control, and so on, but for planning new controls, regimentation and social experiments.

The Senate's ultra-Liberals thereby avoided financial restrictions which the doles from the contingent fund would have imposed. A minor subcommittee, for instance, had a staff whose pay approximated $85,000 a year, virtually all borrowed. Others set themselves up on a similarly ample scale.

As to the legality of the arrangement, there was no question. Such loans were authorized. They became in time, however, a pink annoyance to a dominant coalition of Conservatives, and finally the Senate eliminated the practice.

Truman was good fellow to the Senate's pinko and radical members. But his own committee was not so staffed; its workers were selected for their ability to do a job rather than for their flaming political views. Under this policy, the Truman committee achieved earthy results while some of the other special committees and subcommittees were shooting at the moon.

Truman became involved in their celestial promotions in only one case and then innocently. He stuck to his own job and traveled down no blind alleys. And he was a Regular of the Regulars; he cast his vote for every bill Roosevelt asked Congress to pass in the name of the national defense or the prosecution of the war.

One of these, for which Truman was keen, was the Selective Service Act and the drafting of eighteen-year-old boys. Having a son of sixteen at the time, I protested to him against the low age limit. He was completely unsympathetic. Eighteen-year-old boys, he said, make excellent soldiers, a point quite outside of my protest. The discipline and training afforded them in the armed forces, he added, not only benefited them physically but broadened their viewpoint.

"We all know that," he said. "The only people who object to it are you and a lot of fond mamas."

Some of Truman's cronies wanted the National Youth Administration's life extended for a year. This agency was shown later to have been honey-combed with radical officials and workers. Truman voted for the extension. He likewise voted to extend the life of the National Resources Planning Board whose expensive function from which dividends, if any, yet have to come was to remake America. He broke with Bennett Clark, his colleague, to vote authority to the President to proceed with the St. Lawrence seaway and power development. That was a grant of power Roosevelt had asked for repeatedly and didn't get.

In his second term, Truman continued to live up to his reputation as one of Labor's best friends in Congress. He overlooked the "mere racket" practiced by labor unions selling work permits to laborers at Army construction camps. When it was suggested that the Government draft labor (in September, 1943) for essential war production, Truman pooh-poohed the notion.

"I am here to say," he told the Senate, "that I do not think it is possible to force any man to work unless he wants to work. I do not want to draft industry and labor. I do not think there is any substitute for efficiency and I do not think there is any substitute for a man wanting to do the job he is doing. . . . It is efficiency we must seek and not more complex and unworkable controls."

His sympathetic attitude was toward Labor's rank and file, not its overlords. He had not forgot them; already he had glimpsed a day when they would have to reckon with Congress.

"There is no difference between a labor leader with too much money to spend on an election and Mark Hanna with too much money to spend on an election," he said (January, 1944) in a Senate address.

"I think the time has come when labor unions, cooperatives and similar organizations . . . are going to be required to make an accounting of their funds and of what they do with them, for the benefit of the public and the public interest."

Nevertheless, when it came to a vote, he voted against a proposal that labor leaders be made to disclose what they were doing with their funds. That was embodied in the Revenue Act of 1943; mildly it called for only a confidential disclosure to the Bureau of Internal Revenue and involved no tax. Truman was among its losing opponents.

The Smith-Connally anti-strike bill, affecting Labor's rank and file, came before the Senate in 1943. Truman voted against it; when it was vetoed by Roosevelt, Truman voted to sustain the veto. Each time he was on the losing side. The measure, he thought, was too drastic to accomplish its purpose.

But when he became President he was not slow to avail himself of the Smith-Connally law. Under it he seized, notably, the nation's soft-coal mines when a strike threatened. The powers he voted to deny his predecessor in wartime he exercised himself when he occupied the White House. And at that time the shooting was over on all fronts.

Later, when a rail workers' strike threatened, Truman went before Congress to urge hurry-up enactment of a bill far more drastic than the Smith-Connally law. Again he was on the losing side; Congress declined.

His viewpoint as Senator was not his viewpoint as President.

As Senator Truman, he voted for price control, but he made clear his opposition to lingering controls after the war's end.

"Regulation for the sake of regulation," he told the Cleveland, Ohio, Chamber of Commerce in April, 1943, "is nonsense. The imposition of complicated rules by people who know nothing of the industry they are running cannot be tolerated."

For his committee, he reported to the Senate on March 4, 1944:

"There is too great danger that such controls would become self-perpetuating, especially if the war should last a long time. If that should happen, we would indeed have won the war and lost the peace."

Hostilities were nearly a year gone by when Congress, in June, 1946, sent him, as President, the Price Control Extension Bill, eliminating most of the controls exercised by the Office of Price Administration. Truman vetoed the bill, holding that the time was not ripe then to lift controls. His veto was sustained.

As the war and the defense investigation lengthened— the committee was not renamed but remained officially the Committee to Investigate the National Defense Program—Truman became more confident of his status and surer of his judgment. Gone were the days of his self-deprecation. His fingers lay athwart the public pulse and he was quick to sense popular sentiment.

Early in 1944, I was talking with him one day about the political outlook. That was months before his unexpected nomination as Vice President. I was his "Black Republican" friend in those days, depressed by the prospect that Roosevelt would be nominated for a fourth term.

"If he's nominated," I predicted, "he'll be defeated. I

can't imagine the American people giving any man four terms in the White House."

"Want to bet on that?" Truman asked.

"Not particularly," I replied. "Do you?"

"Yes; I'll bet you a hundred dollars he'll be nominated and elected," Truman said, reaching for his wallet. "How about it?"

"No, Harry," I said. "I don't want to bet. I don't want to take your money."

"Hmpf!" he grunted. "You'd lose, not I."

After the election, I reminded him of the conversation.

"You seemed to be very confident and cocky about it," I said.

"I was," he replied. "I knew the American people wouldn't fire the captain when he was winning the war."

Coming from Roosevelt's running mate, that analysis summed up all there was to say, it seemed. It was pithy, characteristic Trumanese which hit the bullseye with high explosive force. I recall a similar statement he made in the spring of 1940:

"No crackpot's fool enough to take a crack at me."

Such was his comment on a letter threatening harm to him. An unsigned note, scrawled with a lead pencil, it had been mailed at Kansas City when the vote-fraud scandals were redolent. Truman was unconcerned but Messall was disturbed. For months thereafter, at Messall's request, the Washington police had Truman under their protective surveillance. When he went back to Missouri, the Kansas City police watched over him, as did the New York City police when he made an address there.

The writer of the note was never apprehended.

Truman was a busy man and hard to see as his investigation broadened. In earlier days he had had plenty of time to chat when I dropped in at his office. This was no longer so; I often found him rising to terminate an interview when I had more to discuss.

"You're not trying to get rid of me, Harry, are you?" I asked.

"You know I'm not," he replied. "I just don't have time enough to do all the things I'm supposed to do."

Even so, he was never too busy to serve his friends. In 1939, Morris Glazer, editor of the American Trucking Associations' weekly publication, suggested that I ask Truman to address the association at its forthcoming annual meeting at Chicago.

"I'll be glad to do it," Truman said.

"I think they would like to pay you a fee—an honorarium, to be highfalutin," I said.

"I don't want it and won't take it," he answered quickly. "I'm a public servant and public servants have no business charging fees for making speeches on public matters. Tell 'em I'll be glad to go to Chicago and make 'em a speech if they'll pay my traveling and hotel expenses."

And so it was arranged. Truman's attitude was in sharp contrast with the eagerness of several of his colleagues who were glad to get such assignments—at from $300 to $500 each, plus expenses.

Three years later, when Truman was up to his eyebrows in work, the truckmen again wanted Truman to address their annual convention, to be held at St. Louis. Glazer and

John Lawrence, the association's manager, called on Truman and made the request. Again he agreed to do so.

"The last time you addressed us, Senator," Glazer said, "we wanted to show our appreciation with a little financial token. You wouldn't accept it then, but we hope you will this time."

Truman waved him away with a grin. "No," he said, "I haven't changed my mind."

Once I suggested to Truman that his investigation would furnish material for an interesting book.

"I agree with you," he said. "Go ahead and write it; I'll help you all I can."

"All right," I replied, "on two conditions: that you be co-author, and that you share in any compensation."

"I can't do that, Bill," he said.

"Why not?"

"I suppose it would be all right ethically, but I feel that I would be making capital out of my public service, and I don't think I ought to do that."

So that was another book I didn't write.

As the war neared its end, a rising tide of unrest produced many strange legislative proposals. Truman lent his name to only one. That was sponsored by his close friend, Senator Kilgore of West Virginia, and by Senator Murray of Montana. The latter was Chairman of the Senate's Small Business Committee.

The Murray-Kilgore-Truman bill sought to amend the Reconversion Act by substantially increasing compensation for idle workers. At the time of its introduction (1944) the Government's statistical sharps downtown were predicting dire calamities for labor when the war should end. There would be vast unemployment, they agreed. War production plants would close, workers would be discharged wholesale and civilian production would be unready to absorb them. Such was the premise on which they based the forecasts.

Fantastic estimates of unemployment were projected. A leading New Deal economist estimated that the number of unemployed workers would reach 5,000,000 during the reconversion period; others foresaw even greater unemployment. These gloomy predictions, which later proved to be unwarranted, were the cue for political action.

One provision of the Murray-Kilgore-Truman bill called for weekly pay of $25 for each unemployed worker up to a limit of twenty-six weeks. These payments, the bill provided, were to be made largely from Federal funds through the appropriate state agencies administering the Social Security law.

The self-proclaimed author of the bill was an $8,000-a-year employe of the War Production Board named Herbert Schimmel. Schimmel had been loaned by W.P.B. to Murray's committee. Kilgore and Truman discussed the bill and the latter expressed his sympathy for its objective.

Unknown to Truman at the time, the House Committee on Un-American Activities had investigated one phase of Schimmel's previous work that linked him closely to Sidney Hillman's Political Action Committee.

The House Committee had seized documents of the Political Action Committee containing records of long-distance telephone calls between P.A.C.'s New York office and Washington. Eight person-to-person calls, according to the record, were made to Schimmel; and there were others, station-to-station, to Schimmel's telephone extension in the Senate Office Building.

In a discussion with newsmen in Kilgore's presence, Schimmel said most of the calls were between him and former members of a Kilgore subcommittee staff later employed by P.A.C. Those members were identified; Kilgore said they had been loaned to his subcommittee by a downtown agency. A third former staff member, Kilgore said, had left the subcommittee to become a legislative counsel for Philip Murray, C.I.O. head.

Schimmel was asked by newsmen about his connection with the Kilgore subcommittee when it issued a report on war shipping. He said he had served then as chief of the investigations and hearings staff and had supervised the report. That report had been denounced, soon after its issuance, as "A New Mission from Moscow" by the *West Coast Sailor*, official organ of the Sailors' Union of the Pacific.

"The report itself," said the *West Coast Sailor*, "could have been drawn up and submitted by any Communist party front, so faithfully does it perform the functions of the Communist Party."

At that time Truman was the Democratic nominee for Vice President. Immediately after Schimmel's self-admitted authorship of the bill was revealed, Truman told me he had withdrawn his name from its sponsorship. But he still thought the objective of the bill was a good objective.

Before the Senate acted on the bill (S. 1274, 79th Congress), Truman became President. He then sent a message to Congress urging adoption of the program. The bill was passed in greatly modified form after a coalition of Republicans and Conservative Democrats had ripped the $25-a-week-for-twenty-six-weeks provision from its text. The measure then went to the House where it was referred to the Ways and Means Committee.

There it was pigeonholed. Truman insisted upon enactment of such a program and summoned the Democratic members of the Ways and Means Committee to the White House. He told them he wanted them to report out a bill containing the program, so that the House could complete the legislative action. The members of the Committee did not care much for the incident; they had other ideas and the bill died in its pigeonhole.

That bill was of a stripe with legislation proposed by senators whose committees were staffed by the very, very liberal workers from downtown.

The House Committee on Un-American Activities listed these downtown workers of radical ideas and connections who came up to the Capitol to help draft new laws. One measure of that sort, supported by Henry Wallace, was the so-called Full Employment Bill of 1944. A downtown agency employe on loan to the Murray committee was the reputed author of that one.

The notion embodied in the bill was provision for "full employment" for all workers in the postwar period, with Government funds paying the bill where necessary. The bill's declaration of policy was interpreted by coalition senators as a Government guarantee that every worker should have a job.

Truman was in sympathy with the objective, although he did not commit himself as to the bill's details or its guarantee.

The bill's reputed author had a long listing in the files of the Committee on Un-American Activities. According to them, he was a member of four organizations labeled by the committee as "fronts" for the Communist Party. One of these was the Washington Committee for Democratic Action. In the committee's files that organization was listed as the same as the Washington Committee for Democratic Rights.

Here is what the committee's records contain, in part, as to the latter:

"Shortly after the dissolution of the American League for Peace and Democracy"—in which membership was held by the Full Employment Bill's actual author, according to the House Committee—"in February, 1940, the Communist Party set about organizing a whole new series of new front organizations.

"In the selection of names for these organizations, the party displayed a marked preference for those which had the phrase, 'Democratic rights' in them.

"For example, in the Nation's capital, the Washington Committee for Democratic Rights came into being as the principal front organization of the Communist Party. On the national scale, there was set up the National Emergency Conference for Democratic Rights."

The House Committee's records also state that the Washington Committee for Democratic Action "was the local District of Columbia chapter of the National Federation for Constitutional Liberties."

[215]

As to the last-named organization, the Attorney General of the United States (Francis Biddle, at that time) in a "strictly confidential" memorandum sent to his division heads wrote:

"The National Federation of Constitutional Liberties is part of what Lenin called 'the solar system of organization' ostensibly having no connection with the Communist Party but by which the Communists attempt to create sympathizers and supporters of their program among those who would never affiliate themselves openly with the party. . . .

"Its method of operation, like that of the International Labor Defense, the legal arm of the Communist Party with which it is closely affiliated, is the creation of special committees for special cases. . . . The announced program of the Federation shows a close parallel to the Communist Party line in 1940."

The Senate coalition would have none of the Government guarantee of a job for everybody, embodied in the Full Employment Bill. The measure was modified greatly, passed, and sent to the House for enactment. Representative Manasco of Alabama was chairman of the committee that considered it there.

In open hearings, Manasco read portions of the original Full Employment Bill and then read portions of the Communist Party platform. The language differed but the principles were identical.

With further changes, the bill was passed by the House and approved by Truman as President. It was a rather innocuous measure when Congress had finished operating on it, its chief provision being to provide three $15,000-a-year jobs for advisers to the President. The latter were to tell him periodically whether prosperity or dull times were in the offing.

Such was the general background of much so-called liberal legislation sponsored by some of Truman's close friends and sometimes supported by Truman. There was no dearth of social reformers in committee staffs and apparently no limit to their schemes in the last two years Truman served in the Senate.

Truman was unaware of the background of much of this legislation. The House Committee on Un-American Activities was not unaware. It had the record of the indefatigable small fry originating bizarre proposals at the Capitol. It also compiled, and closely guarded from public inspection, a list of members of the House itself who were allied with so-called Communist-front organizations.

These organizations were numbered by scores in the committee's listing. The history of some went back for years. For instance:

"The American League for Peace and Democracy was one of the most effective Communist-front organizations ever operated in this country. In 1939 it was found that more than five hundred officials of the executive branch of the Federal Government were members of the League."

The League disbanded in 1940, the year after the Hitler-Stalin pact was signed. It was not revived. But after Hitler's invasion of Russia, the League had many successors in the United States—organizations of the "rights" and "action" type.

Workers in those organizations followed a pattern in their efforts for radical legislation. The first step in the design was for the worker to be assigned to a "Liberal" committee or subcommittee, preferably of the Senate. That generally was arranged through confederates in the downtown agencies.

Once assigned, the worker diligently cultivated the good will of the committee member for whom he was working. After winning the member's confidence, the next step was casually to suggest the legislation the worker wanted.

After the seed was planted it was nurtured. The member soon would be hearing from friends, constituents, or leaders of movements, notably Labor, friendly to him. A few such endorsements spread with apparent innocence over a fortnight or so would impel him to think again: There might be merit in the idea.

The next step was to discuss it further with the worker who had planted it. The final step was to embody it in a bill.

Among the radical workers at the Capitol there was much rivalry. If one group, for instance, should convince their member that the moon was made of green cheese and Congress ought to do something about it, other groups would try to convince their members they should start something more bizarre. And so the merry game went on.

The ideal of radical craftsmanship was for a worker to convince a member so thoroughly of the need for legislation that the member would come to believe the idea had originated with himself.

The small fry didn't try such tactics with Harry Truman. They tried to work on him through his friends in the Senate. In some cases those friends won Truman's approval of measures spawned in the fertile field of radical imaginings. In others, they won his general approval of objectives of such legislation.

In no case did it appear that Truman knew the origin of the proposals he was informally agreeing to.

For Harry Truman was engrossed in his committee work. One day in the autumn of 1943, when he was fast becoming an outstanding senator, I dropped in for a chat at his office. Harry Vaughan was there, and Hugh Fulton. They were discussing nothing in particular, and I joined in.

"I wonder if you realize what a name you are making for yourself," I ventured. "Your committee is tops and still going."

"Yes?" asked Truman, grinning agreeably. "I'm glad to hear it."

"Yes," I echoed, "and I think, Harry, you'll be going places if you don't watch out."

"What do you mean, Bill?" he asked.

"Well, all you have to do is to keep on like you're going now. Then let the hint be passed around that you wouldn't mind having second place on the ticket next year. I think you could get it."

From his expression, I gathered I had hit him with a new idea. From his reply, I knew he didn't like it.

"Now, I want you to get this straight," he said, almost savagely. "I don't want to be on the ticket. I don't want to be anything except Senator from Missouri. I'm not looking for anything else.

"I'm not going to be nominated Vice President, even if I should be considered for the place which I won't be. The simple reason is I don't want it. I don't want to be

Vice President. I want to be Senator. You're doing me a disservice to mention it. I don't want you ever to mention it again. I've got all the job I want, and that's flat."

I was astonished by his vehemence. Vaughan and Fulton favored me with withering gazes. Truman was so disturbed he rose from his chair. Presently he sat down again and glared at me.

But Harry Truman, I well knew in my amusement over his attitude, was not one to hold a glare. In a few moments he was smiling again.

"All right, Harry," I said. "Have it your way. Have you finished your lecture? May I say something now?"

His reply was to the general effect that I had never failed to speak my thoughts freely when I came to his office.

"Well, what is it?" he asked pleasantly.

"Simply this—NUTS!"

Vaughan and Fulton registered horror.

"Going over to the Senate?" I asked Truman amiably. "If so, may I walk along?"

He was smiling again as we walked through the corridor.

"Really, Harry," I said, "for a moment I thought I had offended you. You gave me quite a start."

He stopped and faced me. I have never seen him more earnest.

"Why should I go on the ticket, Bill, even if I were asked to? I have everything I want here. I don't want to be Vice President. You know that, don't you? Don't you know I don't want to be Vice President?"

Anybody looking into his face would have known it.

"Yes," I said. "I believe you."

And that was that—the first time, I am confident, that Harry Truman heard a hint of his becoming Vice President. Often the incident has come back to me. It never fails to come to mind when I pass the spot in the corridor where he stood. I can see him now, standing there, saying, "I don't want to be Vice President."

Chapter Eleven

———————✳———————

AS THE time drew near for the Democrats to name their candidates in 1944, it appeared that Harry Truman had worried over something that wouldn't happen at all. His fear of the nomination seemed altogether unwarranted. The lightning was flashing away off to the Midwest in the political sky.

A week or so before the Convention, Truman's name was mentioned only occasionally and casually as a possible nominee. And whenever it was mentioned, Truman issued another one of his statements: He wasn't a candidate, didn't want the nomination, had said so often, and this time please make it final.

When the Convention met at Chicago on June 26, the leading candidate was Henry Wallace. He then was Vice President and greatly desired renomination. Under his standard were arrayed the solid ranks of Organized Labor leadership; his Field Marshal was Sidney Hillman, then at the peak of his popularity with Roosevelt. At the Convention, Hillman was Roosevelt's chief lieutenant, and

Roosevelt's instructions were to "clear everything with Sidney."

It looked on the surface as if Wallace would romp away with the nomination. Only a few weak rivals had bobbed up to contest with him. Chief of these was James F. Byrnes, Senator from South Carolina. Byrnes hailed from a section where the predominant Conservatives regarded Wallace as a dangerous radical. Southern delegates blocked the Wallace stampede.

As to first place on the ticket there was no doubt whatever. Franklin Roosevelt had the delegates eating from the palm of his hand. His nomination again as a wartime President was foregone. It lay wholly within his power to name his running mate, as well. He was fond of Wallace and probably would have given the word to nominate him had it not been for the rumble of rebellion from the South. That—probably that alone—made Roosevelt pause.

The states named their delegates to the Convention. When Missouri named hers, they elected Harry Truman chairman by unanimous vote. It was the first time in years that a Missouri delegation had done anything unanimously. Sam Wear, the lawyer who helped Truman win renomination in 1940, was elected vice chairman.

On Friday morning, June 23, when Truman was in Independence, about to leave with his wife and daughter for the Convention, he received a telephone call from Senator Byrnes at Washington.

"Harry," said Byrnes, "I'd like very much to be nominated Vice President. Are you a candidate yourself?"

"No," replied Truman, "I certainly am not."

Byrnes was relieved. "In that case," he said, "maybe

you can help me. Will you? It's all right with the President; he told me it was all right with him if I were a candidate."

"I'm about to leave for Chicago, Jim," Truman replied. "When I get there I'll do anything I can to help you."

Later in the day Senator Barkley of Kentucky, the Majority Leader, tried to reach Truman by telephone to urge his support of Byrnes but Truman had gone.

At Chicago, Truman learned of Roosevelt's instructions to "clear everything with Sidney." He went to Hillman's hotel and they had breakfast together.

"Jim Byrnes wants to be nominated Vice President," Truman told Hillman. "I think he would be an excellent selection. Of course, I know you're supporting Wallace, but if Wallace can't get it, I hope you'll get behind Byrnes."

"Nope," said Hillman, "we don't want Byrnes."

Truman wanted to know why. Hillman said Organized Labor was afraid Byrnes wouldn't give it the support Wallace would; besides, that Byrnes was from the South and Labor didn't want a Southern man on the ticket with Roosevelt.

"All the Labor men feel that way," Hillman said.

"But suppose Wallace can't get the nomination," Truman insisted. "What then?"

"If Wallace can't get the nomination," Hillman replied, "there is only one other man I would support for it."

"Well, who's that?" Truman asked.

"I'm looking at him," was Hillman's reply.

Truman was astounded. "I'm not a candidate," he managed to say. "I don't want the nomination."

Truman then called on Philip Murray, C.I.O. head, seeking Murray's support, next to Wallace, for Byrnes. Murray declined.

The next call Truman made was on his favorite labor group, the leaders of the railroad unions. He saw "Aleck" Whitney who had contributed so substantially to his renomination as Senator in 1940. Whitney had a group with him, all rail union officials. Truman made a plea in Byrnes' behalf. They refused to entertain it.

Truman breakfasted the next day with William Green, head of the American Federation of Labor. Green was as deaf to the Byrnes plea as the others.

As these various meetings and conferences were held, Truman reported the lack of progress to Byrnes.

Meanwhile, Robert E. Hannegan, who had been the main factor in swinging St. Louis to Truman in the primary election of 1940, was openly plumping for Truman for Vice President. Others joined Hannegan. Truman waved them away again and again. He told them the same rote, "I'm not a candidate. I'm for Byrnes."

But they persisted. At breakfast Thursday morning, Senators Tydings and Radcliffe of Maryland spied Truman in the hotel dining room. They came to his table.

"Come over and get acquainted with our Maryland delegation," Tydings said. "We don't want Wallace for Vice President."

"I'll be glad to meet them," Truman said, "but just to get acquainted. I won't do you any good in your trouble, though. I'm not a candidate."

"Well, come on, anyhow," Tydings insisted. "You never can tell what may happen around here."

Truman went over and shook hands with the Marylanders.

Hannegan had been after Truman for days to announce he would accept the nomination. Now he came up again.

"Look here," Hannegan said, "I've got something to show you."

He pulled a crumpled bit of paper from his pocket and handed it to Truman.

"Tell Harry Truman," was scribbled in lead pencil, "that I want him to be Vice President. F.D.R."

"The President wrote that," Hannegan said. "*Now*, will you take it?"

"I don't believe the President wrote it," Truman said. (Later he learned that the note was authentic.) "I think you're just kidding me, Bob."

Senator Byrd of Virginia and Senator Bankhead of Alabama saw Truman. They told him there was a serious revolt in the South against Wallace. Their state delegations and those of Mississippi, Louisiana, Maryland, half of the Texas delegation, and many from other states, they said, would do all possible to prevent Wallace's renomination. There would be a split in the Party, they feared, if Wallace were named.

"If you'll agree to accept the nomination," they told him, "then eventually we'll swing our delegations into line behind you."

"But I don't want it," Truman answered. "I'm for Jim Byrnes."

The Missouri delegation met. Truman was in the Chair. Wear sat at his right hand. A motion was made that the delegation declare for Truman as Vice President.

"The motion is out of order," Truman ruled, "and I'll not put the question."

A ruse was adopted. A delegate went to Truman and engaged him in whispered conversation. Wear jumped to his feet.

"I rule that the motion just made *is* in order. I'll put the question. All in favor——"

Truman looked up, started to rise, sat down to the bellow of a thunderous "Aye."

"*Now,* will you take it?" Hannegan asked again.

"No," Truman told him. "I'm for Jim Byrnes."

"All right," Hannegan answered. "Come over to my suite in the Blackstone this afternoon. I want to talk to you."

Truman agreed. It was Thursday; the Vice Presidential nomination was to be made the next day. Arriving at Hannegan's suite at the appointed time, Truman found a group of leaders. Hannegan was there, expecting him. So were Mayor Hague of Jersey City, Mayor Kelly of Chicago, Postmaster General Walker, and Ed Flynn of New York, former National Committee Chairman.

They started in with arguments to make Truman change his mind. While they were in the thick of it, the telephone rang. Hannegan answered.

"Sh-h-h!" he shouted, waving for silence. "It's the President at Washington."

Roosevelt talked loud and excitedly. Hannegan held the instrument a few inches from his ear. Roosevelt's words were heard by everybody in the room.

"Have you persuaded that fellow yet?" Roosevelt asked.

"Not yet, Mr. President," Hannegan replied.

"Well, what have you been doing all week? This is Thursday."

"Mr. President," said Hannegan, "I've been trying to fix it up. I've been on his neck ever since he got here, but he is the contrariest cuss I ever saw in my life."

"All right," Roosevelt replied, "just tell him for me that if there's a split in the Party he'll be the one responsible for it."

"Wait a minute, Mr. President," Hannegan requested.

Putting his hand over the transmitter, Hannegan turned to Truman. "The President says—"

"We heard him," one of the group interrupted. "We all heard him."

"Did you hear him?" Hannegan asked Truman.

"I did."

"Well, what must I tell him?"

Truman hesitated. "Well," he said slowly, "if he feels that way about it, I guess I'll have to take it."

Hannegan turned back to the phone. "It's all right, Mr. President," he told Roosevelt. "He's just said he would take it."

Hannegan hung up and faced the group. "Whew!" he sighed.

"Well," Truman said glumly, "now I've got a job ahead that I don't like. I've got to tell Byrnes."

When he found Byrnes and told him, Byrnes was mad as a hornet.

"But the President said it was all right for me to be a candidate," he said several times. "I don't get it."

Truman went back to his hotel and broke the news to his wife and daughter. They saw their prospects for privacy fading for the next four years. They felt as he did. It was a gloomy family group.

"I think I'll ask Bennett Clark to put me in nomination," Truman said. "Where's Bennett? Where do you suppose I can find him?"

He found Bennett at his hotel, but it was early the next morning. Bennett, worn by activity and late hours, was hard to awaken; when he did wake up he was still heavy with sleep. Truman ordered a big pot of coffee sent up and for nearly two hours they sat there talking.

That day Clark placed Truman in nomination and he was nominated.

A few days later, Truman returned to Washington and called on Roosevelt. They had luncheon on the White House lawn.

"Harry," said Roosevelt, "I've got to do something for Henry Wallace. He has been perfectly splendid in his loyalty and is going to do effective campaign work for us."

"What does Henry want?" Truman asked.

"He wants to be Secretary of Commerce."

"I think he's crazy to want that job," Truman commented.

"Well, he wants it, and I think I'll give it to him."

"All right, Mr. President," Truman promised, "I'll help you get him through if he runs into trouble in the Senate and I believe he will."

There was something else on Roosevelt's mind.

"You'll have to do the campaigning, Harry," he said. "You'll have to make speeches and go places over the country. When you do this, I have a request to make. Travel by train, don't fly."

"Why not travel by plane?" Truman asked.

"Because one of us has got to stay alive," Roosevelt said.

Truman promised.

He kept his word, both as to train travel and saving Henry Wallace's political hide. For after the election, when Truman was Vice President, a stupendous controversy arose when Roosevelt asked Jesse Jones to resign as Secretary of Commerce and gave the job to Wallace.

There was red-headed opposition to Wallace in the Senate. The fight was so hot and close that in a preliminary test of strength Wallace won by only one vote.

Twice Harry Truman saved Henry Wallace from rejection by the Senate.

The first time, Truman worked for a week to swing opposition senators to support for Wallace. Truman talked with Bilbo and Eastland of Mississippi, George of Georgia, Bailey of North Carolina, McKellar of Tennessee, and others. He won several converts, persuaded one or two others not to vote against Wallace's confirmation if they felt they couldn't vote for it.

That saved the day for Wallace. Without Truman's preliminary work as Vice President, Wallace would not have been confirmed.

On the second occasion, Truman was presiding over the Senate.

Wallace supporters had won votes for their man by agreeing to pass a House-passed measure divorcing the Department of Commerce from the Federal Loan Agency. Under a special law, Jesse Jones had been head of both. The idea was to restore the former situation, so that Wallace would be confirmed as Secretary of Commerce only, so that he would have no supervision over the billions of dollars lent by the loan agency.

Under that condition, some senators who otherwise opposed Wallace had agreed to vote to confirm him as Secretary. But even so, the margin was narrow.

Procedure agreed on was for Barkley to place the House-passed bill immediately before the Senate when it convened. With that bill passed—Roosevelt had given advance assurance that he would approve it—the way would be clear for Wallace's confirmation.

Other senators, led by Taft of Ohio, opposed confirmation under any circumstances.

When the Senate convened, Barkley was slow in getting to his feet. Taft was on his feet like a flash, demanding recognition. He was prepared to move immediate action on Wallace's nomination, before the Senate could pass the saving bill. Truman knew he was on his feet but simply did not see him. He waited a few seconds that seemed like days for Barkley to rise. When Barkley did rise, Truman recognized him and the agreed-upon procedure was followed.

Disappointed, Taft took his seat. Had he insisted on his rights, he could have forced first consideration of the nomination. And there was no doubt that under such circumstances it would have been rejected. As it was, Wallace was confirmed.

For little more than three months, Truman presided over the Senate and thoroughly enjoyed his work and the attendant social life in the capital.

On the afternoon of April 12, 1945, the Senate recessed

at five o'clock. Truman then telephoned Speaker Rayburn, saying he wanted to come over and discuss a pending bill with him.

"All right, Harry, come along," Rayburn told him. "I'm in what they call my hide-out in the Capitol."

Truman sent his car to the House side of the Capitol and walked to Rayburn's hide-out. He found several others there with Rayburn. Before he could discuss what he had in mind, Rayburn told him Steve Early, of the Roosevelt secretariat, had left an urgent message for him by phone. Truman was to come at once to the White House and enter by the front door.

Truman left immediately. He thought the President wanted him to substitute as honorary pall-bearer at the funeral of a distinguished clergyman who had died a day or so before. At the White House, Truman was ushered to an upstairs room in which he found Roosevelt's wife and daughter, Anna, and Early.

Mrs. Roosevelt came forward and put her hand on Truman's shoulder.

"Harry," she said, "the President is dead."

Truman was astounded. "What can I do to help you?" he asked.

"Nothing to help us," Mrs. Roosevelt told him. "That isn't the question. The question is, what can we do to help you?"

High official Washington was summoned to the White House by telephone. Truman himself summoned his wife and daughter. A few minutes after seven o'clock, Truman was sworn in as President.

From that moment, he was President in his own name.

He relied at first on the representations of those who had been close to Franklin Roosevelt. Even then, he decided for himself the major questions of policy cascading upon him.

Members of the Cabinet, as usual in such circumstances, immediately tendered their resignations so that President Truman might be free to select his own advisers. He asked them to carry on for a time until he could make the selections. As he made them, the members of the Roosevelt Cabinet dropped out, one by one.

One of the first was Secretary of State Stettinius. Truman nominated, as his successor, Senator Byrnes of South Carolina. Only a few persons know the impelling reason for selecting Byrnes. It was Truman's desire, so far as he could, to soften Byrnes' disappointment when he failed to win the nomination as Vice President.

Henry Morgenthau, Jr., Secretary of the Treasury, and Henry Wallace, Secretary of Commerce, were among the last of the Roosevelt hold-overs to leave the Truman Cabinet. They did so under unusual circumstances.

Wallace's speech at New York urging appeasement of Russia at a time when Secretary Byrnes was getting tough with the Soviets has been regarded generally as the reason why Wallace resigned. It wasn't the real reason, although it was a prime factor. The misunderstanding had been adjusted by Wallace's statement saying a misunderstanding had occurred. The incident was closed, so far as Truman was concerned, when Wallace called at the White House a day or so after issuing his statement.

"Mr. President," Wallace told Truman, "I am going to

be your Left hand in this Administration and I'm going to do what I can to help you."

Truman thanked him, adding that he didn't relish Wallace's attack on Byrnes.

"Mr. President," Wallace said, "I think the end justifies the means."

Truman immediately saw red. And Red. He recognized the expression, "the end justifies the means," as a cardinal principle of Communist doctrine. It was an argument, Truman felt, that could be and had been used time and again to justify anything—even murder, on occasion.

The comprehension of what his Secretary of Commerce was saying was immediate and demoralizing.

Addressing Wallace by his first name, President Truman said quietly he was sorry to hear Wallace utter such a sentiment. He didn't want a man in his Cabinet who thought that way. The best thing Wallace could do, under the circumstances, would be to resign. Right away, please.

Wallace resigned at once. He had no choice.

That was the reason why. Not because of his inept attempt to undercut Byrnes in dealing with Russia. Not that; but because he had leveled at Harry Truman a line that Truman immediately recognized as coming straight from the Communist Party.

Henry Morgenthau's case was different.

Morgenthau advocated a policy of toughness with defeated Germany. He had wanted to strip Germany of all industry and make her purely an agricultural nation. His ideas had not been accepted. Policy-making in foreign lands was no part of Morgenthau's duties as Secretary of the Treasury, but Morgenthau loved to dabble in it.

[234]

One day Morgenthau called on Truman and suggested that the President take action, which he outlined briefly, as to certain details under the get-tough-with-Germany policy he advocated.

"I want you to do so-and-so," he told Truman.

Truman was astonished. He thought Morgenthau was joking. In a tone reflecting his astonishment, he asked Morgenthau to repeat what he had said.

"I want you to do so-and-so," Morgenthau repeated.

The President then realized that Morgenthau was in earnest and answered emphatically that he wasn't going to do it.

"In that case," Morgenthau said, "I suppose there's nothing left for me to do but quit the Cabinet."

That was right, Truman assured him. He could quit any time—now, if he wanted to.

And so Morgenthau quit.

The last vestige of Harry Truman's self-abasement was gone. His self-deprecation was ended. Harry Truman now was President of the United States in reality as well as in name. He, and nobody else.

Index

Index

Index

Index

Index

Supreme Court, proposed packing of, 50, 98, 142

Taft, Robert A., 107, 231
Taft, William Howard, 35
Tenant farmers, Federal help to, 85
Tennessee Valley Authority, 83, 116
Thompkins, Dr. William J., 135
Tobey, Charles W., 158
Trade Agreements Act, 95, 96
Transportation Act of 1940, 75, 91, 113
Truman, Bess Wallace, 16
   Margaret, 16
Two-term precedent broken, 38
Two-thirds vote ruling, 35, 37, 38

Vaughan, Harry, 13, 14, 84, 130, 219, 220

Vice Presidency, the, 15
Vice President elect, 59ff.

Wade, James R., 129
Wagner Labor Relations Act, support of, 81
Wallace, Henry, 15, 87, 156, 157, 158, 214, 222-235
Wallgren, Mon, 159
War Production Board, 188
Washington *Labor*, 133
Wear, Samuel, 58, 129, 223, 227
Welch, Philip, 129
West Coast Sailor, 213
Wheeler, Burton K., 54, 73, 74, 112
Whitney, A. F., 132ff.
Willkie, Wendell, 76
Wilson, Woodrow, 23, 27, 35, 36, 100
Woodring, Harry, 125
World Court, adherence to, 83